Master of Me

Meditations

Donna Goddard

Copyright © 2025 by Donna Goddard

All rights reserved. No part of this book may be reproduced in any form or by any electronic or mechanical means, including information storage and retrieval systems, without written permission from the author, except for the use of brief quotations in a book review.

Contents

Introduction—All All   vii

Part One
Body and Health

1. Remake Yourself   3
   Gone for Good
2. I Have You   11
   Body Map
3. Crystalline Body   19
   Activating Yin and Yang
4. Clean and Clear   23
   Soften to Source

Part Two
Nature

5. Orchestration of Nature   31
   Tree, River, Heart, Breath
6. Back to Our Roots   37
   Melting Away
7. Mutitjulu Waterhole   43
   It is Done

Part Three
Healing

8. Sparkly-Eyed River   53
   Gathering Grievances
9. Karma Burning   59
   Emotional Release
10. Healing Circle   65
    Healing a Childhood Hurt

11. Healing Injuries and Body Pain   71
    Light Stream
12. Warehouse Meditation   79
    Mind Yourself

Part Four
Peace and Love

13. Becoming Spacious Within   91
    Open Sky
14. Your Life is Perfect   95
    Nothing to Fear
15. Encounters   101
    Exchange of Presence
16. Love Without Edges   105
    The Soft Field of Being
17. Dove's Peace   109
    Melt and Dissolve
18. Giving and Receiving   113
    In Balance
19. Releasing Our Loves   117
    Reaching for the Stars
20. Spread and Share   121
    Pay it Forward

Part Five
Creating

21. Walking Your Way   127
    Life Path
22. Follow Your Passion   131
    Beethoven Frequency
23. Different Realities   139
    Awake and Aware
24. Sand Between Your Toes   145
    Flowing Creation
25. Choosing with Clarity   151
    Crossroads

Part Six
Space and Consciousness

26. Beyond Time — 157
   Loosening Linear Life
27. Shattered Sea — 163
   Reconnection
28. Balance Blueprint — 169
   So Be It
29. Intelligence — 173
   Artificial and Higher Intelligence
30. Mystery — 177
   Finite to Infinite
31. The Journey of Spirit — 181
   Through Life and Beyond
32. Heart — 187
   Love, Truth, Generosity

About the Author — 191
Also by Donna Goddard — 193

Introduction—All All

Seekers, Seers, Teachers

Master of Me: Meditations is for spiritual seekers, seers, and teachers.

We are all all of them.

We are all seekers—though we may not know what we seek.

We are all seers—though we may be looking through a murky window.

And we are all teachers—to someone, in some way.

Naturally, the quality of our seeking, seeing, and teaching deepens with growth.

But that is simply a matter of time (although, in truth, the soul knows neither time nor space).

Every one of us has taken an Earth incarnation to dive deep into the unique human experience of being separated from Source. Once we remember the possibility of return, our homecoming is greatly hastened. It was always assured. However, it is sped up and happified each time we connect with our true nature.

Meditation, in its many varied and marvellous forms, is one of the most direct paths back.

Meditation is not new-age mumbo-jumbo for the ungrounded.

It is intelligent.
It is humble.
And it is powerful.

To meditate is to become consciously alive and well.

It heals the body, clears the mind, and frees the spirit.

In this way, we reduce—and often eliminate—our problems and experience the deep satisfaction of living in an ever-evolving, connected, and creative way.

Set aside time when you can be alone and undisturbed. Dedicate it to your well-being. Some of the meditations in this book are short; others are longer. Sometimes, you only have a minute—or can only tolerate a minute—to turn toward the Light. That's okay.

A minute can save you. It can make a world of difference. It can help you relax, release your worries, and realign with your Divine nature.

Other times, you may settle into a longer meditation—a "proper" session of twenty minutes or more. The nervous system and electromagnetic field often need that long to reach a deeply meditative and beneficial state.

Once you become acquainted with the meditative state of mind, it tends to stay.

And after a while, you become inseparable from—and deeply in love with—the consciousness of love that underlies all authentic meditative practice.

You become a walking, talking meditation yourself.

Part One
Body and Health

Chapter 1

Remake Yourself

Gone for Good

This meditation takes you back in time so that you can remake your life according to your deepest desires and wishes. It will help your body relax, your mind settle, and your energy system calm and energise itself.

Settle in an upright position, either on the floor or in a chair. Lean your lower back on something if you need to. If you want to lie down, that's okay too.

- Breathe in deeply. Breathe out. Relax, relax, relax. Relax your body.
- Breathe in. Breathe out. Relax your mind. Feel that you're giving your mind total permission to relax.
- Breathe in. Breathe out. Feel that you're allowing your whole auric field to relax and settle.

Time Travel

In your mind's eye, picture yourself as you are **now**. You're looking at yourself, your appearance, what you consider your good points, and what you feel could be better. Look at yourself with your current personality, lifestyle, and everything that's in your life at the moment. Look at yourself quite objectively.

Now, we're going to go back **one year**. It doesn't matter if it's not exact. Imagine yourself one year ago, around this time. Remember what you were doing and where you were living. What sort of things were happening? Great things, things that were not great, remember all of it. It's quite safe to do so. Go back one year ago and see where you were, the clothes you wore, what you were doing, what was happening, and who was in your life. Look at yourself closely.

And now we're going to go back **five years.** Remember what age you were five years ago, where you were living five years ago, what you looked like five years ago, who was around you five years ago, and how you felt five years ago.

We are going back **ten years**. Whatever your age was

ten years ago, visualise yourself then. Picture exactly what you looked like ten years ago, your body dimensions, what sorts of things you were doing ten years ago, how you felt in yourself, the things that stressed you, the things that made you happy. It's safe to go back and see it all.

Go back to when you were **ten years old.** See what you looked like and how you related to your family, schoolmates, and teachers. What were your problems? What brought you joy? What made you cry? What were your dreams when you were ten years old?

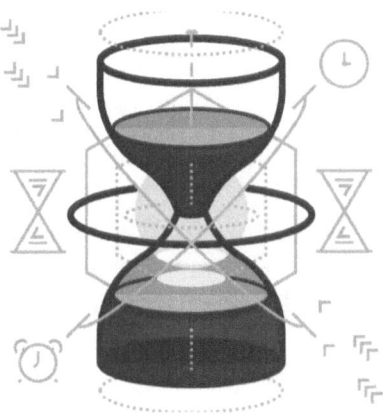

Now, go back to when you were **one year old**. You're picturing yourself as a one-year-old child. Picture where you lived when you were one. You're a one-year-old child. See yourself toddling around as a one-year-old child. Look at yourself. See what you looked like. What would you have been thinking about when you were one year old? Did you feel happy? How did life look to you? Were you glad to be here? Were you confused? What was the energy of your family like? How did they relate to you?

Go back to when you were a **newborn baby**. You were

just born, a brand-new baby being pushed into the world. Go inside that tiny body. What does it feel like to be in that little body? What does it feel like to be in the world?

And go back before that to when you were just a **few cells**. That's all you were, a few cells in your mother's body. You were there, but only a few cells. Was your spirit there, or were you looking on from somewhere else?

Reach Out, Let Go

Make sure your eyes are closed. See a being in front of you. It is a highly relevant spiritual teacher to you, usually the first one that comes to your mind, someone you trust 100%. The being is standing near you, watching over you. They reach their hand out to you, and you reach out to them with your energy body. They're going to pull you out of this world and this human life. When they do it, you will utter a deep guttural sound from your throat. It's the sort of sound people make when they die. Whatever sound comes to your mind will be appropriate for you.

Get ready. Hold their hand. And GO! Let them pull

you out of this world. And as they do it, make that deep sound in yourself. Feel them pulling you away. Release yourself to the process. You are totally safe. Let go. Let go. Let go.

Gone

You are now gone, in a different place, no longer on Earth. You're back in the dimension you were in before you came here. You have your spiritual guide, mentor, and protector with you, and you're safe.

You don't have any cells. You don't have a body. You don't have a human personality. See yourself as having no personality. You don't have a mind. You don't have human thoughts. You have no preferences. You have no desires. You have no ambitions. You have no thoughts, personality, mind or desires but are a valued energy. You are an entirely valuable energy. You feel peaceful. Getting there wasn't so peaceful, but once you're there, you've let everything go for a little while. Enjoy being there because there's no pain of any sort. You're in a protected space.

If there's something you would like to ask your teacher, ask them now and see what they have to say. Ask whatever you'd like to ask.

A few minutes to listen to the teacher.

Return and Remake

The teacher has given you the ability to remake your life when you return to Earth. On the way back, you're going to remake yourself at all the different ages. You're going to remake your energy field in a way that you want to make it.

As you go back through the years, you will undo all the karma you don't want to carry. You're remaking yourself, and you have your teacher's blessing to help you do it.

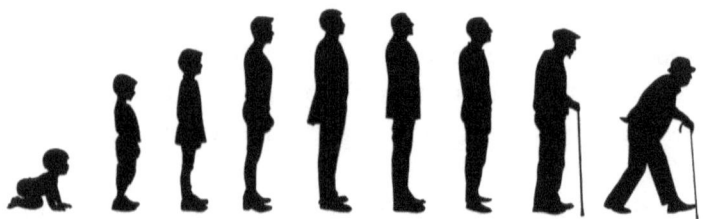

Ready? Return to your mother's womb as a **few cells**, and remake yourself there. Only bring what you truly want with you. You can leave behind all the mistakes, all the bad karma, all the pain that you no longer wish to hang onto. You're not bringing it with you. You're remaking yourself.

You're now being born. Remake yourself as a **newborn baby**. You know exactly how you want this life to go. It's a great privilege to be here. You're pleased to be here and will make your life entirely as you wish it to be. There are little spots of light inside you. They are all the talents, abilities, loves, and intentions you've brought. You intend to make those lights grow brighter and brighter. You have everything you need inside you to do that.

You're now **one year old**. See yourself toddling around with the energy field you want to have. Any time you feel a stumbling block in your remaking process, a bit of trouble, or something bothers you, let it go and keep moving forward.

Keep rebuilding yourself through the years as they speed by. You are now **ten years old**, a revamped ten-year-old you. Imagine how you want your ten-year-old self to be. See the best possible version.

You're now **twenty-one**. Look carefully at your young adult self. Ensure they think, act, and be how you want them to be. Observe the decisions you are making as a twenty-one-year-old. Get rid of anything that you would no longer choose. You're remaking your whole energy system as a twenty-one-year-old.

Travel to **five years ago**. Make sure that person is the version of you that you have decided is the right version of you. See how that person behaves and watch how other people respond to them. Look carefully and thoroughly, and remake yourself.

Come back to this **present moment**. Know that you have the power to make the rest of your life absolutely how you want it to be. Anything that you have an interest in, anything that you're drawn to, anything that you feel you're capable of contributing to your own life, your family's life, and the lives of the people around you is doable. You have the ability, energy, and drive to do it, and you can draw to you what you need. You have remade the karma you originally brought with you or inadvertently created so that it's not dragging you back. You have a clean energy field. You've cleaned yourself out.

You'll gather more karma, and some of it will sneak back in, but you've given it a beautiful clean. Some of it will not return or be recreated. You got rid of it. It is gone for good.

Chapter 2

I Have You

Body Map

This meditation invites you to inhabit your body with warmth, clarity, and respect. Rather than treating the body as a mere vehicle or a problem to be solved, we'll treat it as a wise companion—alive with signals, steadiness, and joy. The aim is not to force change but to listen so deeply that the body reveals its natural ease.

Settling

Find a position that feels both supported and alert. Sit upright on a chair with your feet on the floor, or lie down if your body needs that today. Let the spine be long without strain; let your face be soft. Breathe in slowly. Breathe out completely. Again, breathe in. Breathe out and allow the shoulders, belly, and jaw to release what they don't need to hold.

Let your attention rest where the body meets support —feet with floor, hips with seat, back with cushion, body with bed. Feel the ordinary, reassuring fact of contact. The body knows how to be held by gravity; it has done so since your first day here. Let gravity do its job. You don't have to carry yourself all alone.

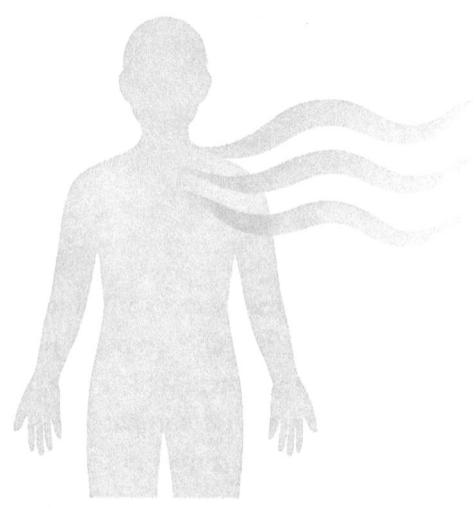

Posture and Breath

Imagine your spine as a flexible column rising from the base of your pelvis to the crown of your head. Don't rigidify it. Allow it to be buoyant, as if gently lengthening with each inhalation and settling with each exhalation. Place one hand on your belly and one on your chest. Notice which moves more. Invite the lower hand to receive the breath first, the upper hand to follow. No force—just a patient re-training toward deeper, kinder breathing.

Breathe in... let the breath widen the ribs and soften the belly.

Breathe out... let the breath empty without collapsing.

Continue for a minute, letting the breath become an anchor, a tide, a friendly rhythm you can trust.

Ground and Gravity

Shift attention to your feet (or the parts of you that are in contact with support if you're lying down). Sense the architecture of your feet—the heel, the ball, the toes, the arches. If you're seated, let the weight travel down through the legs into the floor as if roots are growing, subtle but real. If you're lying down, imagine the ground rising to meet you, shaping itself to your curves, saying: "I have you."

Notice how the rest of you organises around this grounding: the pelvis getting heavier, the breathing more generous, the back less defensive. Let the floor be trustworthy. Let the chair be trustworthy. Let the Earth be trustworthy.

Mapping the Body

We'll scan the body slowly, not as a checklist but as a conversation. Bring curiosity, not criticism.

Begin at the crown of the head and feel the scalp, forehead, and temples. Let the forehead smooth; let the eyes settle deeper into their sockets as if resting in warm water. Notice the tiny muscles around the mouth and lips; invite them to soften. Sense the back of the neck and the base of the skull, where effort often hides. Let the throat feel spacious and unblocked, as if breath could move behind it with ease.

Travel down through the collarbones across to the shoulders. If you find tightness, don't fight it—place a friendly attention there, the way you'd lay a hand on the shoulder of someone you love. Move down the upper arms, elbows, forearms, wrists, and hands. Let the hands grow warm and open. The hands know how to receive and to release; they can teach the heart both skills.

Return to the chest and back. Let the ribcage be like bellows—widening to the sides and back, not just forward. Sense the shoulder blades gliding on the back as the breath moves. Visit the heart space without stories, just presence. Down through the solar plexus into the belly; imagine the organs like a quiet lake—buoyant, supported, unhurried. Into the pelvis: feel the bowl of the pelvis holding you from beneath. Let the hips be heavy and kind.

Move through the thighs, knees, shins, calves, ankles, and feet. Notice what wants more space, what wants less. The scan is complete, but not finished; it will continue in the background, adjusting you gently as you rest here.

Rivers of Sensation

Now we'll feel for subtle currents. Imagine two rivers of sensation flowing in you: up the back of the body on the inhale, down the front on the exhale. Inhale—up the back from tail to crown. Exhale—down the front from throat to belly to pelvis. No precision needed; this is not a technique to get right but a way of encouraging circulation and ease. Ride these rivers for a few breaths and let them find their own pace.

Clearing and Nourishing

If there is a place that calls for attention—an ache, a pull, a tense spot—bring your breath there as if you were breathing right through that area. On the inhale, offer space. On the exhale, let warmth and heaviness drain down toward the ground. If a gentle micro-movement would help—a tiny tilt of the pelvis, a small roll of the shoulders, a slow turn of the head—allow it. Let the fascia and muscles take their time. The body responds to kindness more than to command.

If it helps, hum softly on an exhale to let vibrations travel through the tissues. Humming can gather scattered effort and encourage release. Try a few relaxed hums and feel the resonance settle places words don't reach.

Strength and Softness

The physical is not only about letting go. It is also about awake tone—strength without hardness. Imagine a line of quiet strength running from the arches of your feet up through the inner legs, through the pelvic floor, along the front of the spine, to the crown. Not a brace, not a posture you have to hold, but a living line that supports you from within. Around that line, let everything unnecessary soften. Strength at the core, softness at the surface.

Senses as Gateways

Open the senses lightly, one by one. Hear the sounds in the room and beyond, without labelling them. Feel the air on your skin, the temperature and movement. Taste what's in the mouth; smell the subtle scents around you. Open the eyes and soften the focus, taking in light and shape without grabbing. Let sensation be simple. When the senses are allowed to be present without demand, the nervous system settles and the body's natural intelligence rises.

Embodied Intention

Place one hand on the heart and one on the belly. Ask the body, not the mind: "What do you want me to know today?" Wait. A word might come, or an image, or a feeling, or simply a deep exhale. Whatever arrives, receive it without judgment. If no answer comes, trust the question to keep working in you.

Walking Practice (Optional)

If you have space and it's comfortable, stand slowly. Feel the transfer of weight into your feet. Begin to walk at a natural pace, a small circle in the room if needed. Let the breath and steps find each other—nothing dramatic, just everyday walking with unusual kindness. Notice how the body organises: the heel touching, the roll through the foot, the quiet propulsion from the hip, the swing of the arms, the balance of head over spine. Let walking itself be the meditation: grounded, ordinary, sacred.

If you're lying down or seated and prefer to remain, imagine this same walking from the inside, a rehearsal of ease that the body can later inhabit.

Return

Come back to stillness. Sit or lie down as you began. Breathe in softly. Breathe out completely. Feel again the simple facts: contact with support, the length of the spine, the warmth of the hands, the steadiness of the feet. Sense how the body now feels more like home than an object, more like a friend than a task.

When you are ready, open your eyes. Let the rest of your day be conducted from this inhabiting—strength without hardness, softness without collapse. The physical is your companion, not your limit. Walk with it. Listen to it. Let it shine.

Chapter 3

Crystalline Body

Activating Yin and Yang

This meditation will connect you with the energy lines running down the front and back of your body. It will assist in balancing and activating yin and yang energies. In Traditional Chinese Medicine and energy practices like qigong and acupuncture, the **Governing Vessel** runs along the spine on the back of the body. It starts at the perineum (the point between the anus and genitals) and runs up the midline of the back, over the head, and ends at the upper gum behind the upper lip. The **Central Meridian** runs along the front midline of the body from the lower lip to the perineum. Both lines are crucial for the flow of energy in the body.

Energy Lines

Relax your hands on your legs, or wherever is comfortable, with your palms open and facing up.

- Breathe in and up the Governing Vessel. Start at the perineum, travel up the midline of your back (spine), over your head, and down to your upper lip. Breathing in and up the Governing Vessel activates yang energy, which is expansive and lifting.
- Breathe out and down the Central Meridian, which runs down the front of the body from the lower lip to the perineum. Breathing out and down the Central Meridian activates yin energy, which is grounding, calming, and nourishing.
- Again, breathe in and up the Governing Vessel from the perineum, up the back spine, over your head, and down to your upper lip.
- Breathe out and down the Central Meridian, from the lower lip, down the front of the body, to the perineum.
- Breathe in and up the back spine, over your head, to your lip.
- Breathe out and down the front of the body from the lower lip to the perineum.
- Breathe in, back of body.

- Breathe out, front of body.
- Breathe in, back body.
- Breathe out, front body.

*Breath is the power of life,
the essence of your being.*

Body In Mind, Not Mind in Body

As you continue to breathe, see your mind, consciousness, or soul expanding with each out breath. Let your energy body grow more each time you breathe out. Think of yourself as a giant, translucent ball of shining energy. Watch as your spread and size slowly increase. You are full of light and getting bigger and bigger.

A tiny shape is in the centre of the massive ball of light. It is the shape of a human body, your body. Contrary to normal perceptual belief, your mind is not inside your body. It is the other way around.

Your body is inside your mind.

Crystalline Human

The human form, which is in the centre of the large ball of consciousness, is crystalline. It has a clear, ordered internal structure with cells that form crystal-like patterns. Energy from the large ball of Higher Mind has been condensed and distilled into a tight, static, smaller ball of crystalline human body. When the body "dies," the crystalline substance reverts to Higher Mind.

The crystalline material that forms your body can be

reformed differently. Whenever you expand your consciousness and move your energy beyond your body's boundaries, the material of the physical body can restructure itself more healthily.

Imagine your crystalline body in perfect health. Nothing is grating or clunking. Everything is operating smoothly like an oiled machine. Your body is silent and strong. The yin and yang of your body are balancing themselves. Have a clear image of your body in perfect health, and then, with your consciousness enlarged, imprint that on the crystalline substance that forms your body.

When you are ready, return to your normal consciousness. Retain awareness of your increasing capacity to imprint health on the crystalline body, which has taken form in the middle of your expansive, creative mind. Your Higher Mind forever remains attached to Source.

Chapter 4

Clean and Clear

Soften to Source

This meditation will help you clear your chakras and enliven your energy field so that it sparkles with invigoration and unboundedness.

Humming Bee

Stand straight with your feet apart. Close your eyes and breathe in. Breathe out. You're going to make a continuous humming sound on your out-breath. Start at your crown, go down your whole body, and then come back up. While humming, mentally scan your entire body. Ready? Go.

- Breathe in. Hum while slowly breathing out. Scan down your body. Then, scan up your body.
- Take a breath in and repeat. Hum down your body while breathing out. Then, scan up.

- Feel that, as you hum, everything in your body is correcting itself. You are humming and scanning your body.
- Breathe in. Breathe out and hmmmm. Down and up.
- Breathe in. Breathe out and hmmmm. Down and up.
- Breathe in. Breathe out and hmmmm. Down and up.

S-Shape Release

Stay standing. It is time to clean your energy system using a repeated S-shape down your body. Use energising and pumping music to assist in this process if you like. It will add some beneficial fire.

1. Join your hands in namaste or prayer position and place them above your head.
2. Beginning at your crown chakra, make a semi-circular movement to your third eye.
3. Continue making S-shaped movements down your body through your throat,
4. heart,
5. solar plexus,
6. sacral,
7. root or base chakra,
8. knees,
9. and feet.
10. Then swoosh the unwanted energy away! Think of releasing everything in your body that doesn't make you well and happy.
11. Repeat for as long as feels good to you.

Start at the crown and move through the third eye, throat, heart, solar plexus, sacral, and root chakras. Then, continue through your knees and feet, and OUT of your body with a swoosh.

Bead on a String

Sit down and settle. Imagine that you are a bead on a string, and the string is your spine.

1. As you breathe in, move up your spine like a bead sliding up a string. Move from the base of your spine to the top of your head.
2. As you breathe out, move down your spine like a bead sliding on a string. Move from

the top of your head to the base of your spine.
3. Breathe in and move the bead up your spine.
4. Breathe out and move the bead down your spine.
5. In and up.
6. Out and down.
7. In, up.
8. Out, down.

The bead is loosening as you continue to breathe in and up, out and down. The bead is your personal mind.

- Your mind is changing from dense, solid matter to a pliable material. Your personal parameters are softening.
- It is now changing from a pliable material to a liquid. Its boundaries have enlarged, and it is looser.
- As the bead dissolves, it changes from liquid to airy gas and becomes much bigger.

- The gas escapes all its parameters and travels further and further away from your spine.

Nothing is holding you back. You move ever outwards until you become so light and transparent that you are no longer visible. Your personal mind is melting into universal consciousness or Source. Allow yourself to melt. Keep softening yourself more and more. Soften all your thoughts. Soften all your fears. Soften all your worries. Let yourself disappear.

You will still have an individual identity, but it will not be made of personal mind. It will be made of spirit consciousness, which is vast and limitless. There is a power far greater than us that is running life. Wherever you are, right at this minute, whatever is happening, whatever your relationships are like, whatever state your money is in, whatever your health is doing, whatever pains you've got, whatever happinesses you have—all of it has expanded and merged with Source. You are not insisting on anything. You're letting be, joining with Life. There is no need for worry, anxiety, or anger. What's there to worry about? What's there to be afraid of? What's there to be angry about? You are part of the flow of creation and eternally safe and secure.

When you are ready, blink your eyes several times and open them.

Part Two
Nature

Chapter 5

Orchestration of Nature

Tree, River, Heart, Breath

This meditation will connect you to the Earth. You are part of the Earth. When you connect to it, you connect to yourself. Syncing with nature is necessary for our physical and energetic health. It also opens communication gateways with our higher self and other dimensions. Take time out every day (or at least once a week) to be in nature. You'll find it tremendously helpful in strengthening your connection with the force behind life.

Ground Level

Take one long, deep breath in, and as you breathe out, feel that you're sinking into the ground. Take another breath in, and as you breathe out, feel that you release everything you no longer wish to hold onto.

On Track

See yourself walking down a beautiful forest track. It is the beginning of autumn. You can see a hint of the first leaves turning colour, but only a hint. The leaves are shining brightly and moving around in the breeze. Some have a silver backing, turning backward and forward like majestic tinsel in the sunlight. Although it's a warm day, it's cool on the track because the trees make a shady covering. It feels very pleasant. The gravel track makes a crunching noise as you walk—crunch, crunch, crunch, crunch.

Next to the track is a creek. It gurgles along, jumping over rocks, sliding around tree trunks and river grasses, dancing here and there, taking the path of least resistance. Bubble, bubble, bubble, bubble. As you walk along, the creek skips along beside you.

As Solid as the Earth

You come to a magnificent tree. You know it's an oak tree because you can see acorns lying on the ground. Most of them are still green, as they are the early fallers. The tree has a mesmerising, powerful quality emanating from it. It is partly covered by green ivy. The ivy is not suffocating it. The tree and ivy are in balance. It is a beautifully picturesque scene.

Something tells you to stop at the oak tree, which is situated between the track and the creek. You take a few steps off the track and look both ways to see if anyone is around. You haven't passed a single person all the time you've been walking.

You sit next to the tree facing the creek and lean your back on the wood of the trunk. It feels so solid and old, as if nothing could phase it. It has seen people and animals coming and going. It is as solid as a rock, as solid as the Earth.

Listen

Sitting cross-legged with your back against the oak, you look at the bubbling, happy creek. And you listen. At first, you don't hear much, but then you hear the oak tree leaves moving in the wind. The wind picks up intensity and starts moving the leaves more. It seems that the wind is playing with you. The rustle of the leaves gets louder and louder—swish, swish, swish.

The movement of the leaves is syncing with the gurgling, bouncing creek—bubble, bubble, bubble. The leaves and creek are moving as one, creating a musical beat —swish, swish, swish, bubble, bubble, bubble.

Another instrument of nature's orchestra enters—your heartbeat. Ba-boom, ba-boom, ba-boom. Your heart syncs with the leaves of the tree and the dancing creek. All three are aligned—your heart, the moving leaves of the tree, and the dancing creek—swish, swish, swish, bubble, bubble, bubble, ba-boom, ba-boom, ba-boom.

Then, a new instrument joins the orchestra—your breath. Breathing in, breathing out. You watch your breath. You listen to your breath. It syncs with the rest of the orchestra, breathing in and breathing out gently and calmly. YH (inhale), WH (exhale). Gently and calmly. YH-WH, YH-WH, YH-WH. All four aspects of nature are in unison —tree, water, heartbeat, breath—swish, bubble, ba-boom, YH-WH. Swish, bubble, ba-boom, YH-WH.

Power Prism

Tree, water, heartbeat, breath—swish, bubble, ba-boom, YH-WH—combine to form a square. Push out the square to make a prism. As the form becomes larger, it includes more and more of the nature around you.

You breathe out carbon dioxide, and the tree breathes it in. The tree breathes out oxygen, and you breathe it in. You breathe out, and the tree breathes in. The tree breathes out, and you breathe in. As this rhythm continues, you become more bonded with the tree. Your spirit travels into the tree along with the carbon dioxide—into the leaves, along the branches, down the trunk, and into the roots.

The oak tree roots are connected to all the other tree roots along the creek. There is an entire root city underground, busily transferring food and water and communicating with each member. Drink deeply from the clean water in the creek. You are drinking the clean water through the tree's roots. It will make you well, whole, healthy, beautiful, happy, creative, expressive, intelligent, calm, and on fire with ideas.

All is one great orchestra. You not only see, hear, and feel it, but you are it. You are the orchestra of Earth and all that it contains.

It is you.
It is you.
It is you.

When you are ready, slowly open your eyes.

Thank you to the creek.
Thank you to the tree.
Thank you to yourself.

Chapter 6

Back to Our Roots

Melting Away

This meditation will unite you with your higher etheric roots and your grounded Earthly roots. Both are essential for a full human experience.

Pat-Pat

Lie down, close your eyes, and breathe in. Hold your breath. Breathe out. Do this again three times slowly. In, hold, out. In, hold, out. In, hold, out.

Rest your arms beside your body, palms facing down. Breathe in and then pat the floor or bed several times with your palms as you breathe out. Repeat two more times. Breathe in and breathe out while patting the bed. In, out, while patting the bed.

Triangle Temple

Turn your palms to face upward. Focus on your right palm and feel a ball of energy in it. Let the energy ball grow to a couple of inches. Keep your attention on it for about thirty seconds.

Focus on your left palm and feel the energy growing. Keep your attention there for about thirty seconds.

Focus on your third eye, the middle of your forehead, between your eyebrows. Feel that the etheric thumb of your spirit guide is pressing lightly on your third eye. It is slowly, slowly, opening. You can see a tiny ball of light growing to a few inches.

Focus your attention on your right palm again, then on your left palm, and then on your third eye. You're making a triangle. Do it again: right palm, left palm, third eye.

This time, as you do it, move the triangle out to one foot from your body. Right palm: one foot out. Left palm: one foot out. Third eye: one foot out. Trace the triangle in your mind—right palm, left palm, third eye, one foot out from your body.

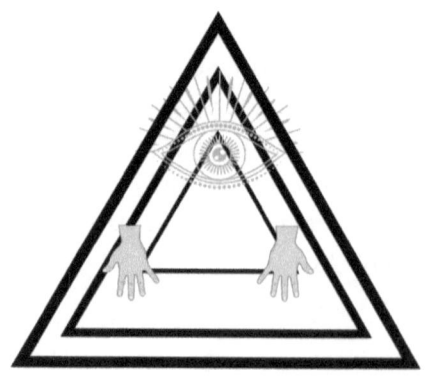

Push the triangle out to ten feet from your body. Ten feet from your right palm. Ten feet from your left palm. Ten feet from your third eye. You are making a large triangle of energy, and you are right in the middle of it. It's a temple. You are the centre point of the temple. You are utterly, entirely safe.

Push the triangle out to one hundred feet from your body. One hundred feet from your right palm. One hundred feet from your left palm. One hundred feet from your third eye. It's a large, energetic triangle. All of it is safe. It is energised. You are in the middle of it.

Melt

In this safe space, your body and mind expand.

- Your feet melt into the bed.
- Your calves melt into the bed.
- Your thighs melt.
- Your stomach, hips, and buttocks melt.
- Your chest, back, and shoulders melt into the bed, to the floor, through the Earth, and into the ether.
- Your neck melts, and your head becomes lighter and lighter.
- Put your attention on your jaw and invite it to relax.
- Focus on your thyroid at the bottom and front of your neck. It's like a butterfly, spreading its wings and becoming lighter.
- Feel the finger of your spirit guide on your left temple. All the muscles and cells in your left temple relax. Then, feel their finger on your

right temple. All the muscles and cells in your right temple relax.

Crystal Water

In this sacred temple, crystal water runs through the entire space. It runs through you. The cleansing water enters your third eye, moves to your left temple, and clears the blockages and stuck points away. It now moves to your right temple, clearing away all the blockages. The healing water runs behind the back of your eyes and makes your eyes feel clean and light.

The crystal water moves to the top of your head, to your crown, forming a ball of energy, and then moves itself in a swirling circle. It moves a foot above your head and makes an infinity sign (a figure eight on its side). Now it comes back to your crown and slowly, very slowly, like honey, starts running down the back of your head. As it travels down, it relaxes every muscle and every cell. It gets to the base of your head, where your skull meets your neck, and stays there. It forms a round ball and moves around, clearing the energy.

Your body is completely relaxed. There is space inside. Your mind has expanded into the one hundred feet of the sacred temple. Your body has become loose and light, and your mind has become spacious and translucent.

Garden

Picture yourself in a faraway garden. You are delighted to be there amongst the trees and the gorgeous energy. Feel the peace. It is incredibly comforting. Look at the wonderful trees, flowers, and growing food.

Sit cross-legged on the soil. It feels warm, soft, and damp. Take your left hand and dig a small hole in the earth. Touch the roots. Beneath the soil surface is an extensive, complex, intelligent, and powerful root system. Dig deep into the earth with your left hand to have closer contact with the root system. You can feel it healing you.

Make a small hole with your right hand. Dig deeper so that you can have more contact with the roots. The root system transfers its healing energy to you. It is synced with you to give balance and harmony. It removes all the energetic waste products from your energy field.

Pain-Free

You remember that you chose to come to Earth. You wanted to experience the pain, pleasure, confusion, and wisdom that Earth people go through. You chose to come here so that you could help elevate the consciousness of the planet. Although you came to Earth to experience things as Earth people do, you do not want to keep the negative in your system, or it will make you sick. Earth can be a tumultuous experience, and you must be careful not to start disintegrating like many Earth people do. You are safe and can have a pain-free existence. You do not have to take suffering into your body, mind, and energy field. You do not have to hold onto anything.

Use your wellness, creativity, and spirit for your benefit and the planet's benefit. Your light does far more than you are aware of. It is helping to reform the civilisation and culture of Earth. You are happy and in no pain. You feel a creative fire inside you. You know any negative experience is temporary and can be healed and eliminated simply by remembering who you are. The vast energy system constantly cleans and helps you. It reminds you of your immense connectedness with the Universe. Listen to it often.

It is now time to return to Earth.

Chapter 7

Mutitjulu Waterhole

It is Done

This earthy meditation will powerfully merge you with nature. From this solid basis, you can create and manifest what you truly want in your life. Become the maker of your destiny.

AUM

Close your eyes and say A-U-M slowly and purposefully. Pay attention to the sound reverberating around your body. Repeat—Aaa-Uuu-Mmm. One more time—Aaa-Uuu-Mmm. Let your natural breath continue. Your body is settling. Your bottom is settling into the chair or the floor. If you are lying down, your body is sinking into the bed. Your entire body, mind, and energy field are releasing themselves to the flow of life. Breathe in. As you breathe out, let your being sink deeper.

Wiggle, Wiggle

- Wiggle your toes, and then stop wiggling.
- Wiggle your feet and ankles, turn them around in circles, and then relax.
- Tense your calf and knee muscles, and then relax.
- Tense your thigh and glute muscles. Relax.
- Tense your chest muscles and heart, and then relax.
- Tense your back and shoulder muscles. Relax.
- Tense your arm muscles. Stretch them out, and stretch out your fingers. Tense, tense, tense, then relax.
- Tense your neck, the back of your head, the top of your head, and your face. Scrunch up your face. Then, release and relax.
- Breathe normally.

Ever-So-Perfect

Imagine you are in a beautiful garden, the sort of garden you would love to be in. It is perfect. The temperature is just right. The sun is shining down, melting into your head, and loving you. There's a gentle breeze, and it's an ever-so-perfect temperature. It's as if the breeze is blowing *through* you, and your body is disappearing in the breeze.

- Your etheric body is gently moving upwards, away from your physical body. It's **a foot** above the ground.
- You keep moving up. Your physical body is clearly visible below. You're about **10 feet** above the ground and can see the entire garden.
- Now, you're at **100 feet** above the garden. You have a stunning view of the garden and the surrounding district.
- You're at **1,000 feet.** It's cool up here, but you don't feel cold because you're in your etheric body.
- You're getting lighter and lighter. You're at **5,000 feet**. It's the height at which some small planes fly. You're up there in the small plane channel.
- Once you reach **10,000 feet**, you start moving horizontally. You're moving purposely because you're going to travel a long distance. Moving, moving, moving—quickly and purposely.

Uluru

Your etheric body has a particular place it wants to go—Uluru, in the middle of Australia. It is a giant red rock. You're moving very fast and can now see that enormous rock on the horizon. It's so far away that it looks like a little red dot. The little red rock is rapidly getting bigger, bigger, bigger, and bigger until you're very close to it. It's about 1,000 feet high, which is not that high. However, its height seems striking because it protrudes from a flat terrain.

Once close to it, you have access to the great etheric library, which holds the records of the universe. It shows you that Uluru is the tip of a vast underground rock formation, like the tip of an iceberg, a rockberg (berg means mountain). The rock formation extends 3 to 4 miles underground.

You assume that you will land on the top of Uluru, but you don't. Slowly, you descend, down, down, down, down. You land at the base of Uluru next to the Mutitjulu Waterhole. Fortunately, the gates have been closed to the tourists. It's the end of the tourist day. The only people who are around at this time of the day, in the late afternoon, are the

Anangu Aborigines who live in the area and are the caretakers of Uluru.

Honey Wisdom

An aboriginal man and his family are near the waterhole. They don't look like the modern Aboriginal people. They look like, maybe, 150 years ago. None of them has Western clothes on. The man has ochre smeared on his body. The family is in a wickiup, a simple structure made from branches and bark. He is standing in front of the wickiup next to a fire and invites you over. Next to the fire is a coolamon, or shallow wooden bowl carved from a eucalyptus tree. In the bowl are pieces of honeycomb. He offers the honeycomb to you with gestures. It's delicious! As you swallow it, the honey feels like tiny golden balls of wisdom entering your body.

Cave

The aboriginal man leads you to the waterhole—the Mutitjulu Waterhole. There's a cave behind it, and he wants you to go inside the opening. He motions for you to go in, but he will remain outside the cave.

You sense that someone is inside waiting for you. Carefully walking through the dark entrance, you see a large, flat rock at the back of the cave. Sitting on the rock is a light being, a master. He is sitting there, silent, still, radiating light.

The master is someone significant for you to connect with. You must decide who the master is. It could be someone you know as a living person or someone who once lived. It could be someone you don't know. It could be an archetype, an elemental, or an entirely etheric being. Use your intuition to know who it is.

You walk up to them and sit on the cave floor. As you watch the master, their light gets brighter and very white—gold and white. An opening in their third eye expands. White light emerges from the master's third eye and is directed into your third eye. You feel it travelling into you. Let it move into all the cells in your head and through your brain and the back of your head. The white light moves into your eyes, throat, and heart. It makes your heart open and soft. It travels down into your belly, making it feel stable and quiet. It moves down your arms and legs. The light touches all your chakras, and you are lit up inside.

Maker of Your Destiny

1. The master asks you to think of something you want to accomplish in the next **2 to 3 months**. Whatever pops into your mind is appropriate—something you would like to achieve in the next few months. Let it form in your mind. Allow it to surface. The master says, "See it as done."
2. Next, the master asks you to think of something you want to accomplish in the next **2 to 3 years**. Whatever you instinctively want to achieve in the next few years is fine—something important to you. And the master says, "It is done."
3. Lastly, the master asks you to think of something you want to accomplish in the next **20 to 30 years**. Make sure that this big vision is inclusive and will serve and bless other people. See it as a light coming from the cave, reaching many people. And the master says, "It is done."

Gently Repeat

We're going to move through those three things again gently. Use a soft focus, not hard, deliberate attention. Think of what you want to actualise in the next 2 to 3 months, and see it as done. In the next 2 to 3 years, see it as done. In the next 20 to 30 years, see it as done.

Know that you can accomplish whatever is in your heart, mind, and soul—whatever desires you would love to accomplish. You have all the energy in the universe to create this. The master then says, "If you have something in your body—your physical or mental body—that you would like help to release, see it as done."

Return

The master's energy starts to lessen. They pull the energy back into themselves and fade. The aboriginal man, the Mutitjulu Waterway's guardian, waits at the cave entrance. You move out of the cave, and he smiles at you. You smile at him and gently lift into the air, travelling up and up. Up, up to 1,000 feet. Up, up, to 10,000 feet. You move horizontally, travelling quickly. As you travel, you remember the beautiful blessings, everything you would like to do, everything you would like to heal, and everything you would like to help others with. You see it all as done.

You're above the garden, coming down from 10,000 feet—down, down, down. You land in the garden and are fully back in your body. Sit with your thoughts for a moment, and when you are ready, open your eyes. *It is done.*

Part Three

Healing

Chapter 8

Sparkly-Eyed River

Gathering Grievances

This meditation will help you to let go of some of your gathered grievances, which will, in turn, transform your life into one of existential prosperity and peace. Existential prosperity is the ability to do what we need to do when we need to do it.

Throw Yourself

Settle your body and whole energy system. We are going to go into a deep practice. Be 100% committed to it. Tell yourself that you will do the practice wholeheartedly. It is a valuable opportunity to release some debris and damaging energy that has gathered inside. Negative energy makes us sick and unhappy. Our spiritual path is a process of getting rid of it to become lighter and brighter.

Getting There

You are walking along a sandy path edged with trees that have been around for hundreds of years. They are hugely tall and straight. It's quite dark because the trees are so big, but it's not disconcerting. It feels friendly. The trees know that you are meant to be there. Anyone who comes on this path is meant to be there. Keep walking, walking, walking.

Sparkly-Eyed River

You come to a river. It is a blue river that shines like people with sparkly eyes. It's called *Sparkly-Eyed River*. When you touch it, you notice the water is cool. You take off your shoes and socks or sandals, put your feet in the water, and walk along the river's edge, paddling in the shallows.

Gradually, you go deeper, and the water is now up to your **knees**. It's a sandy river, much like the path you were on. Keep walking into the water. It is up to your **thighs**. It's not like getting into a relaxing warm bath. The coolness reminds you that you are here for a reason. The water is now up to your **hips**. Keep going further in. It is up to your **waist**. Keep walking. Up to your **chest**. Keep going.

You look around. There is no one in sight. It's only you. The water is up to your **neck**. You falter momentarily but sense that this sparkly-eyed place is safe, and you will be able to breathe under the water. With all your faith and belief that something loves you and will protect you, you keep going. You walk into the middle of the river, and your **whole body**, including your face, is underwater. You find that you can indeed breathe easily.

Channel of Consciousness

You come to a channel in the middle of the river and decide to follow it, deeper and deeper. About ten feet of water is above your head. Then, you arrive at a large rock on the riverbed floor. Crossing your legs, you sit on the rock, not floating up, staying there as if an invisible force is gently weighing you down. You breathe comfortably and wait.

Green Liver

A tiny, green light appears in the distance. It is travelling through the water towards you. It quickly reaches you and enters the top of your head, your crown. Moving down your spine, it enters your liver, in the middle of your body, on the right. It doesn't feel particularly comfortable because it is there to stir up all the resentment in your body. It's stirring it up now. It feels rather unpleasant, but it's not painful. Stirring it up. Stirring it up. There's a lot of it! The green light starts moving in a whirlpool around your liver.

It's going round and round, faster and faster, gathering all the little, big, hidden, and proud resentments. You see them flying past. Big and little, little and big. They're all twirling around in the whirlpool, going faster and faster. The green light pulls them in like a tornado, getting tighter and smaller. Tighter and smaller, until everything from the liver has been pulled into one tiny, green pearl ball. The ball starts moving out of your liver and slowly travels up your spine, millimetre by millimetre.

Space for the green ball to travel up your spine.

AUMing It Out

The green, pearly ball is in your throat. Bring it up a bit higher so it is at the intersection of your mouth and throat. You are going to say one long AUM slowly. As you say it, feel that you're spitting the green ball into the Sparkly-Eyed River. The river will dissolve it in its own way. You may spit out the ball immediately in the first moment, or it may take several AUMs to get it out properly. Take a deep breath. AUM. Repeat, if needed, AUM, AUM.

Say AUM slowly and mindfully.

Love Holds No Grievances

When ready, jump off the rock and swim to the top of the water. You can see the sun shining brightly when you break the water's surface. You feel lighter and cleaner. Something in you has gone. Although gathering grievances is usually inevitable as a human, being on the spiritual path means you are willing to let them go because it's your freedom. It's your way out of suffering. You don't want to suffer. You want to prosper and have peace.

Chapter 9

Karma Burning

Emotional Release

This emotional release meditation will help you feel freer and calmer. Your energy centres will become more activated, invigorated, and enthusiastic as you throw grief, anger, sadness, and broken dreams into the karmic fire.

Settle Down

Make yourself comfortable. Settle into your body. Your bum is securely sitting wherever it's sitting. It's stable and not going to move. Your spine is straight but not tense. Your head and neck are upright in a composed, uncomplicated way.

Fire Up

Your energies are awake and alive, but you need a bit more fire in your body because you are going to burn some karma. To get the fire, you need more oxygen. This process will give you more oxygen. If you feel light-headed, it's okay.

Imagine that you are walking up a mountain.

- At the bottom, it's not too steep. You are breathing through your nose, more deeply than usual, as you've already been walking for a while.
- You come to a small creek. Rolling up your pants, you wade through the water. You have to push through it so you breathe more heavily. Don't fall in the creek. Someone just slipped. I hope it wasn't you. Keep going. You are now safely on the other side.
- The climb is getting steeper. You start breathing in through your nose and out through your mouth.
- You've come to a thicket with many close trees that you must scramble through. You push the bushes apart. It's hard work. You are now

breathing more heavily through both your mouth and your nose.
- Once through the thicket, you approach the last section of the climb. There are many large boulders that you have to scale. Be careful not to slip. A fall would be dangerous at this point. You're nearly at the top, so don't worry about how deeply you have to breathe.
- You can see the top and climb through the gap in the last of the boulders.

Make sure you have spent the last few minutes gradually increasing your breath.

Tip Top

Finally, you're at the top. It's flat, thank goodness! Let your breath settle. You're wandering around and see a fire in the distance beside a cave. Your breath is still settling. It's not stable yet. It's cold at the top of the mountain, although you are hot from the climb. Nevertheless, you walk to the fire and sit cross-legged in front of it. While sitting there, you realise that this fire is the *Karma Flame*. You intuitively feel that your etheric body wants to move out of your physical body and hover a foot or so above the fire.

Your etheric body asks you for permission to move out of your physical body. When you are ready, say yes. Your physical body is now sitting motionless like a lump of earth. It's an earth body, a blob of clay, functioning perfectly but empty without a spirit. Your etheric body is above the flames of the fire. It doesn't get burned.

Karma Flame

Take this opportunity. Throw anything that pops into your mind out of your etheric body into the Karma Flame. Throw in everything you know is damaging to you.

1. Grab your **grief**. It could be grief about anything—death, relationship failures, or anything that fell apart. It could be deaths from other life experiences or other dimensions. Throw it into the fire and watch it burn.
2. Take hold of your **anger.** Let the memories of anger come out of your etheric body—every time someone hurt you, insulted you, ignored you, rejected you, or abused you in any way. Don't worry whether it was true or not, whether someone meant to hurt you or not, whether it was in your mind or someone else's. The karmic mind can't tell the difference. Let it all sizzle out of your etheric body into the raging fire.
3. Let all your **sadness** bubble up inside you, every tear you ever cried. Drop by teardrop,

they are flowing into the fire. The tears hiss on the flames. Let all the memories of hurtful things done out of ignorance, malice, or jealousy expand and rise. Memories of anyone who has hurt you (intentionally or unintentionally) are forming and moving. You are not hurting people by throwing memories in the fire. You're destroying the karma of hurt, which is a burden to you and others.

4. Every broken **dream** you've ever had and every fulfilled dream you have materialised is asking to be released and burned up. Burn it all up—good and bad, every dream that went haywire, every dream that partied all night—throw it into the fire.

Use as much time as you need to do this process. Remember that you can come back later to burn up more karma.

Down and Out

Bring your etheric body back into your physical body, which is still sitting motionless beside the fire. Your etheric body is floating back into your earth body through your three dantians or centres of wisdom (the third eye), love (your heart), and vitality (your lower centre). Your physical body and etheric body have joined together again.

The weight of the two bodies becomes very heavy, and you start sinking into the earth right through the middle of the mountain. Down. Down. Down. Down. Down. You're at the bottom of the mountain but still inside it. Move sideways out of the mountain to where you started your journey. You are now in the sunshine and fresh air. You feel lighter and calmer. Your energy centres are more activated. You are ready to face the world—envigorated, enthusiastic, egoless, and smiling.

Chapter 10

Healing Circle

Healing a Childhood Hurt

In this meditation, we are going on an inner journey to heal a childhood pain.

Close the Door

Find a quiet place to sit or lie down. Close the door and give yourself a little time when you won't be disturbed. Breathe in slowly, deeply. Breathe out slowly, deeply.

Go to the place within where you feel your soul resides. Let that soul part of you rise above your body. Rise higher and higher to the ceiling. Look down at your physical body. You can see your body lying or sitting safely. It will wait for you. It has nothing to do.

Guides

You will need a guide for your journey because, otherwise, you won't know where you're going. On your left and right are two beings. They are angelic beings. They may have taken human form, but you'll recognise them as divine because of their high level of loving goodness and capacity to protect. They have great power, which the Divine bestows on them. They do not need to speak as they communicate telepathically, and you understand instantly what they want to say.

On the Move

You move away from your house, up, up, away from Earth. You don't feel cold or hot. The wind is rushing past you. You feel comfortable, as there is an energy field around you and the two angels. There is a long journey ahead. So, relax.

Few minutes for calm breathing while you travel.

You are now approaching a different land. It resembles Earth and has a blue, shining river surrounded by green grass and majestic trees. It's a very serene and harmonious environment.

You land safely about twenty feet from the river. The landing is soft, and the sun is warm. You sit on the grass and hear the river rustling and bubbling over the stones.

Crossing the River

After a while, you walk to the river. There are ten large, flat stones you can use to cross the water. The rocks are spaced just wide enough to jump from one to the other. Tall, straight trees surround an open space on the other side. They form a wall around a large circle. It feels safe, although mysterious. It feels like something is going to happen, something important and mystical, something that makes you nervous.

Out From the Dark

You notice a figure standing between two of the tallest trees. They have their back to you. You can't tell if they are male or female, young or old. You look intently because you feel that you know them. They slowly turn around. It is someone from your childhood.

It's not an easy meeting because this person is someone you have unresolved issues with, someone who hurt you, although perhaps they also loved you. It's a safe place to meet them here. Nothing bad can happen in this ring of trees. The person has not come to hurt you but to heal and clarify things.

They ask if it's alright to come closer. As you know that the person cannot harm you, you say yes. They slowly walk towards you. You look at them piercingly and notice everything. They look the same as when you knew them as a child. But looking at them from this perspective feels very different.

Time to Speak

They want to discuss the unresolved wound inside you that hurt you. It would be good to have it deleted from your system. It is time for you to speak. There is no need to hold back. This is a safe environment. You explain to the person how you felt about what happened. Whatever you want to say, you can. If you wish, you can swear, cry, stamp your feet, or hurl things around, and the person can accept it.

Space for communication and emotional release.

It is now their turn to speak. Without judgment, you listen to them.

Space for listening.

You understand what is inside them that made them act the way they did. For the first time, you see something you didn't see before. You see the frailty, fear, and hopelessness.

Having both spoken, it is time to leave each other. It might not be a finished story, but something has changed. There is an honesty and a directness that wasn't there before. The person disappears, and you are alone in the forest circle.

Into the Deep and Back

Walking back to the river, you feel the water drawing you into it. You dive under the water and swim deeper. As you are in your etheric body, there's no need to breathe physically. Something in you is different, more peaceful, more whole. There is a serene, soft, beautiful feeling in and around you. It feels light and balanced. There is a natural equilibrium. Everything is in its place. Your heart is bright and alive. Part of you wants to stay there forever, but your other world is calling you back. So, you slowly surface.

Loved and Needed

The two angels return and wait at the river's edge. They tell you that it's time to return to Earth. Once home, they ensure that you are fully back in your body. The angels disappear, but the healing is still there. You are ready to re-enter the world with less burden, pain, fear, anger, and guilt and more wisdom, power, and love. You return to a world that both loves and needs you.

Chapter 11

Healing Injuries and Body Pain

Light Stream

When it comes to injuries, people must do whatever is physically and practically appropriate for them. However, the physical is a representation and demonstration of the non-physical domain. This meditation examines the mental, emotional, and spiritual elements, which are extremely powerful in healing, but don't insist on healing. The body heals when it has the opportunity and the right spirit to do so. Allow, don't demand. All we need is the intention to elevate our frequency.

Privacy

It's important to set aside uninterrupted time when meditating. Ensure you are alone and will not be disturbed. Meditation brings up a lot of mental refuse within our system. If you are worried about people entering the room or other people's needs, you won't allow things to come up, as you will not have the space to deal with them. If they don't come up, they can't heal.

Straight Spine

Settle into your position, either sitting or lying. If you're sitting, it's best to have a straight back. If you're on a chair, sit up straight but comfortably with your legs uncrossed. If you're cross-legged on the floor, sit up as straight as possible. Otherwise, you can lie on the ground, bed, or lounge, but keep your spine straight and your body untangled.

Breathe

Become aware of your natural breathing rhythm. Watch the breath in. Watch the breath out. Breathe in. Breathe out. Keep breathing rhythmically. Let your breath become a little longer, but don't force anything. Allow your body to settle and relax. You are giving your entire system space to sort itself out.

Body Awareness

- Become aware of your feet. Move them around a little, and then relax them.
- Put your focus on your calf muscles, your lower legs, and your knees. Move them around, and then relax.
- Tense your thigh muscles and your upper legs, and then relax.
- Move your hips around, back and forth, forwards and backwards, side to side, round and round. Tense, and relax.
- Tense your stomach, pull it in, and relax. Pull it in again, and relax.
- Tense your chest, wiggle it around, rotate it, move it side to side, forward, backward, and then relax.
- Move your neck and head gently around, side to side, and then relax.
- Tense your arms. Move them in circles. Relax.
- Stretch out your fingers. Make a fist. Hold. Let go.
- Tense your face muscles. Scrunch up your eyes, nose, and mouth. Lift your cheekbones. Move your mouth in a circle. Scrunch up all the muscles in your face, and then relax.
- Breathing in. Breathing out.

Stream of Light

Picture a stream of light above your head. It's touching the top of your head, quietly knocking, saying, "Let me in. Let me in." Visualise the top of your head gently opening to allow the light into your body. It travels down your spine, through your legs, arms, fingers, toes, and out again. This stream of light, running through your body, is your assurance that whatever comes up in this meditation is within a safe environment. The light keeps you safe and is your connection with Spirit. It supports your body's billion functions, large and tiny, which operate without your assistance.

Look At Me

You are relaxed and supported by Spirit, who created and nurtures you. Look deeper into your being. Allow one distressing thought or memory to come up. It could be major. It could be minor. As this meditation is for healing injuries and body pain, you could focus on a thought that is potentially associated with your injury or pain.

Whatever memory comes up is acceptable. Whatever stressor presents itself is fine. Have a look at it. You'll know which particular thing to focus on because it will already be in your mind. If not already shouting at you, it will be tiptoeing around whispering, "Look at me. Look at me. You need to look at me." We must examine ourselves, delve into ourselves, and not live in ignorance of what we think and feel.

At some point, you will have an emotional reaction to the rising thoughts and memories. If you've honestly let an issue come up, you will start to feel something.

Anger, Sadness, Fear

Anger, sadness, and fear are the three main emotional areas that feed our problems.

1. If it's **anger**, be angry. No one is around. Do what you want. Express whatever you want to express. You might be surprised at how angry you feel and what images flash through your mind. This is a safe place to do it, so let it rip. However angry you feel, let it come up. It won't destroy you. You're protected by the light running through your body, which has connected you to the whole of creation.
2. Maybe that's not the type of memory you have. It could be a sad memory. If it's **sadness** that comes up, then be sad. Let yourself cry. Don't stuff your sadness down into some dark layer of your being. Life has many types of grief. It doesn't have to be someone dying. It could be someone leaving. It could be that something has

left your life, something you valued. Learning to deal with grief when it happens and not accumulating karmic suffering in your body will help turn you into an empathetic and whole person. When people do not deal with grief properly, they become depressed, afraid, unable to move, and lacking courage.
3. The other area is **fear.** If the memory coming up has to do with fear, look at how scared you really feel. Fear is our inner child speaking. We have to give it times when it can speak, when it can be angry, when it can be sad, and when it can be afraid. Let yourself be scared. It will pass. Fear is an uncomfortable feeling. It makes us feel vulnerable. However, when we look at the fear and acknowledge it, it helps it to dissipate. We come out the other side.

Each time you do this meditation, you can think of different, specific issues and memories. It is very beneficial to dedicate time to some healing stages or periods in our lives when we can consecutively work through several different issues.

Level Up—the Other Half of the Job

You are now ready to go to the next stage of healing. Sometimes, simply seeing the connection between injury/pain and thought is enough to heal it. The injury/pain becomes unnecessary because the underlying mental equivalent is now seen.

Other times, healing takes longer. Once you have the mental material behind your pain, it is time to level up and elevate your consciousness. Otherwise, you've only done half the job. Seeing the problem and recognising the mess that's inside is only half the issue. The other half of the healing process is to connect deeply with the spiritual and energetic domain.

Bigger Than Us

It doesn't matter what your spiritual beliefs are, which religion you belong to, or if you are an atheist or agnostic. Whatever you see as that which created life, whatever you see as bigger than yourself, more than yourself, that is the pivotal point of protection and healing. If you have a strong connection with a spiritual organisation or church with specific words, books, and teachers, talk to yourself with those words and concepts. That's what you are most aligned with.

We must learn to see ourselves as part of the Divine. The light that came into our crown and moved through our body and limbs is always with us. That light is what made us. We did not make ourselves. Something other than ourselves created us into this magnificent human creature. If we align with it, see it more clearly, understand its possibilities more profoundly, and feel some of its capabilities, we will become stronger, healthier, more whole and loving. What made the universe is a phenomenal, incomprehensible energy. It's much more than you. It's much more than me. It is a vibrating, healing, positive, and joyous force of infinite capacity.

If we ignore the Divine, our progress will be slow. It can take a long time, many lifetimes, for us to improve significantly. We need to listen to the life force, understand that we are part of it, and let it help and heal us so that our potential is fulfilled in a beautiful and thriving way. All of these things happen by paying attention. Healing and happiness go together, and they belong to you.

Chapter 12

Warehouse Meditation

Mind Yourself

Understanding how our mind works is pivotal to living life the way we genuinely prefer. Our mind does not have to be a mystery. It is knowable and usable.

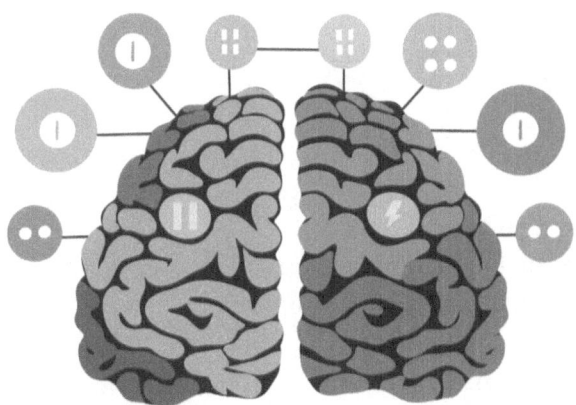

There are three main parts of our mind or consciousness:

1. There is the **conscious** mind, which is a tiny part of the entire mind. It is all the things we usually think about and are aware of.
2. There is the **unconscious** mind, which is the vast majority of our mind. It holds an enormous amount of information, data, and experience, but we are unaware of its contents.
3. The **subconscious** mind is the doorway or gateway between the conscious and unconscious minds. It allows thoughts, memories, and awareness to move from the unconscious to the conscious mind. This is important for many reasons, one of which is healing. A lot of what needs healing in humans doesn't get healed because it's not even recognised as something that needs healing.

Give Over

Take three deep breaths.

- In. Out and relax.
- In. Out and relax more.
- In. Out and relax completely.

Give yourself over to this time. It will help you move forward in some way that will benefit your life.

Metaphors

In our meditation, the large warehouse is your **unconscious** mind, the small shop front is your **conscious** mind, and the person who looks after the shop front is your **subconscious** mind (the gatekeeper between your unconscious and conscious mind).

Front Up

Imagine that you are walking down a road. There is no one about, just you. It's a tranquil place, with many trees along the side of the road. You have a specific place you're going. It's a warehouse, a storehouse. You get to your given address and walk down the footpath to the front of the building. The warehouse is vast, and in front of it is a small shop.

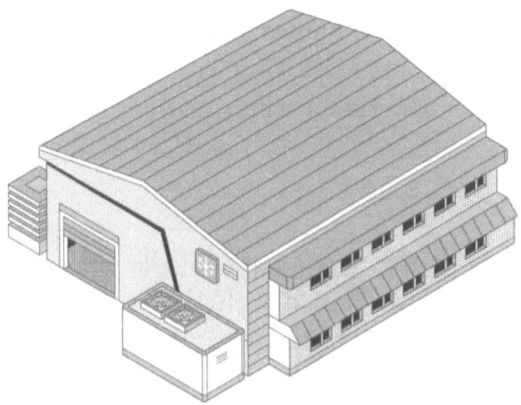

You knock on the door and wait for someone to open it. Finally, someone comes. It's an old man, hunched over and a bit grumpy.

The gatekeeper lets you into the shop, and you look around. The room has many interesting things, but you are there to investigate the large warehouse, your unconscious mind. After a while, he beckons you to the warehouse door. Inside are aisles and aisles of boxes, crates, and containers of all different sizes. Some are very old and look like they've been there since time immemorial. Some are modern and new. They're all muddled together, and you wonder how the gatekeeper could know where anything is.

Relevance

Walking down the warehouse's middle aisle, you notice something strange about the gatekeeper. He seems to be getting younger. His posture is improving. He is taller and now has soft brown hair. His facial expression is no longer angry. It is calm.

On pondering that there must be millions of boxes and containers holding goodness only knows what, you ask, "How on earth do you ever find anything in this warehouse with so many unlabelled boxes?"

"Even though all these boxes and containers belong to

you," says the gatekeeper, "they're not all *relevant* to you at this moment. Some are relevant to previous lifetimes or parallel realities, and some are not yet relevant."

"How will I find the ones that *are* relevant to me?" you ask.

"The boxes will call you," says the gatekeeper, disappearing down one of the aisles.

You're left alone in the warehouse to walk up and down the middle aisle and along some side aisles. You don't know what you are supposed to be looking for.

Inside the Box

You hear a humming sound in the distance. It's humming in your brain as much as from some unseen object. You follow the sound to a back section, which looks similar to all the other sections.

One of the boxes is vibrating, so you carefully remove it from the shelf. It's not too heavy or too big to handle, but you can feel its weight. You're a bit nervous about opening it, but you will because there's something important in it—

a message, something to unravel and discover. Taking a deep breath, you pull apart the top of the cardboard box and see what is inside. What do you see? Whatever it is, it is meant for you.

- Is it a memory, perhaps good, perhaps bad?
- Is it an idea or a thought?
- Is it a feeling?
- Is it a dream?
- Is it your future beckoning you?
- Is it your past haunting you?
- Is it a voice from a galaxy beyond?
- Is it a message from deep within Mother Earth?
- Is your body talking?
- Is your heart crying?
- Is your soul rejoicing?

Take a moment to discover what is inside the box.

Spinning and Spiralling

Whatever is in the box now transforms into a round light, a ball of energy. The energy ball lifts out of the box and rises, of its own accord, to the level of your face. You look inside the white, pulsating energy ball, staring into its depths so that you can draw all its meaning into your mind.

Suddenly, the white ball of light blows apart! KABOOM! It goes in all directions. Thousands and thousands of tiny bits of white light swirl around, spinning, spiralling, twisting, and whirling. With a loud hum, all the pieces come back together and funnel into the top of your head. It travels:

- through your brain and pituitary gland
- through all the cells in your head, face, and neck
- into your thyroid (front of neck)
- down your spine
- into your heart, through all the chambers of your heart
- out of your heart and into your organs
- lungs
- stomach
- pancreas (behind the stomach)
- liver
- gallbladder (beneath the liver)
- kidneys and adrenal glands
- intestines
- bladder

The energy continues to move:

- down your legs
- through your feet
- back up your legs
- down your arms
- into your hands
- back up your arms
- and settles in your throat

Once in your throat, it talks to you and says something significant. Listen to what it's telling you. It's telling you to understand something, to know something, to let go of something, to build something, to love something, to release something.

Space to listen for the energy ball's message while it is in your throat.

"I see the box is empty," says the gatekeeper, who has returned. "Let's put it away."

He takes the empty box and puts it at the back of the warehouse.

"It is time to return to the shop front," he says.

Walking back to the warehouse entrance, you notice the gatekeeper getting older and more curved in stature. He loses his hair, and his facial expression turns grouchy again. By the time you're back in the shop, he's back to the grumpy old man you first encountered.

"Get rid of you, then," he grumbles. "Be gone. You've had enough time."

Delivery Collected

You walk back to the road and feel happy as you have collected your delivery of wisdom and insight. An extra energy now lives in you and is there to help you when needed. You know you can return to the warehouse whenever you need to look for something else. You know how to get there, and someone is waiting to assist you. With that thought, you travel the road happy, relaxed, worry-free, and full of hope and love.

Part Four
Peace and Love

Chapter 13

Becoming Spacious Within

Open Sky

This meditation will guide you into a calm and expansive relationship with your mind. Instead of wrestling with its activity, you will learn to sit within it, observe it, and gently shift its atmosphere. By doing so, the mind becomes not a cage but an open sky.

Settling

Find a position that feels both alert and comfortable. Sit upright if possible, so your breath has room to move freely. Breathe in slowly. Breathe out completely. Again, breathe in, and as you exhale, let your jaw soften. Breathe in once more, and as you breathe out, let the area around your eyes relax.

Bring your attention to the flow of thought. Don't try to control or change it. Simply notice that thoughts are present, like birds moving across the sky. Some fly past quickly; others circle for a while. There is no need to chase them. You are the one watching.

The Watcher and the Stream

Picture yourself sitting beside a gentle stream. The water is clear, moving steadily, always onward. Imagine that each of your thoughts is a leaf placed on the surface of the water. Some are large leaves that stay visible for a long time. Others are tiny, disappearing almost at once.

As each thought arises in your mind, place it gently on the water. Watch it float downstream until it is out of sight. Continue this until you feel less entangled with your thoughts, more like an observer than a participant.

If a thought feels sticky or heavy, don't fight it. Place it on the stream anyway. Watch how even the heaviest leaves are carried by the current.

The Sky Above

Now lift your attention upwards. Instead of the stream, imagine the wide, open sky. Thoughts become clouds—sometimes thick and dark, sometimes thin and bright, sometimes barely there at all.

Notice how the sky is not troubled by the passing of clouds. It remains vast, silent, and unbounded, no matter what drifts through it. Feel that you are the sky. Your mind's surface may be clouded at times, but your essence is the spaciousness in which all thought comes and goes.

The Still Point

Bring your awareness to the centre of your forehead, between the brows—the place known as the third eye. Imagine a soft point of light glowing there. Each breath you take feeds this light. With every inhalation, it brightens. With every exhalation, it grows calmer and steadier.

Let this light fill your mind-space, as though the walls of thought are gently dissolving into radiance. Stay here for a few moments, resting in the still point, nourished by light, held in clarity.

Return

When you are ready, take three deeper breaths. With the first, feel the air entering your lungs fully. With the second, feel your body supported where you are sitting. With the third, become aware of the room around you.

Your thoughts may still move, as they always will, but you now know them as leaves on a stream, as clouds in a sky, as forms moving through spaciousness. The mind is not your prison. It is your companion. And you are free within it.

Chapter 14

Your Life is Perfect
Nothing to Fear

Your life is perfect.
You have nothing to fear.
Everything is fine.
There is nothing to worry about.

You are safe.
You are loved.
You are surrounded
by Divine light.

Don't worry, my friend,
everything is fine.
Relax, relax.
Relax your body.

Breathing in, breathing out.
There is nothing
to worry about.
Release, release.

You do not have
to keep thinking,
with your thoughts
going round and around

through the million
channels of the mind.
There is nothing
to worry about.

Let it go.
You are safe.
Tomorrow you can
think again.

You are safe.
You are in the arms
of the Divine.
You can trust that.

You are always safe.
Peace, peace,
breathe in,
breathe out.

You are your soul,
what you were
before you were born
and after you pass on.

Your soul is safe
in an ocean of love
with countless other
souls, all loved.

Life is one
great harmony.
Everything is in order.
Your life is in order.

Everyone you love is safe.
See them as safe.
See the Divine light
leading them forward.

Despite any picture
to the contrary,
they are
supremely safe.

Nothing and nobody
can take that from them.
They are safe.
They are loved.

You are safe.
You are loved.
Your life is perfect
exactly as it is.

All is in place.
Everything is unfolding
as it needs to.
You are growing every day.

You are opening
to the spirit of evolution.
Tell yourself
that tomorrow

you will be a bit better,
a bit more open
to learning,
to let the light in.

Your life is perfect.
You are special
to the Divine.
You are dearly loved.

Chapter 15

Encounters

Exchange of Presence

This meditation will guide you into the felt sense of meeting another person—not only as a social exchange but as a moment of truth, resonance, and reflection. Every encounter carries the potential to remind us who we are and what we are becoming.

Settling

Sit comfortably, spine relaxed but upright, hands resting where they fall easily. Close your eyes if you wish. Breathe in slowly. Breathe out completely. Again, breathe in. Breathe out and soften the shoulders. Allow the breath to become natural, unforced. Let the body feel steady.

Preparing the Space

Imagine yourself in a simple, open space. It may be a room with plain walls, a quiet garden, or an empty stretch of land. The space is uncluttered, free of distraction. Its emptiness is welcoming, as though it exists only for this moment. You are here to meet another, but first, you prepare the atmosphere—grounded, calm, receptive.

The Arrival

Now imagine a figure approaching. It might be someone you know, or someone unknown. Don't try to decide who it should be. Allow the presence to form naturally. Notice how they appear—how they walk, how they hold themselves. Observe without judgment. They are simply arriving.

When they reach you, both of you pause. Feel the quietness of the moment before any words are spoken. Notice the subtle exchange already happening—the posture, the breath, the energy.

The Exchange

As you continue to sit with this presence, become aware of what awakens in you. Perhaps warmth, perhaps nervousness, perhaps openness, perhaps resistance. Notice without pushing it away. Every encounter brings something to the surface.

Now breathe with them. Imagine that as you inhale, you receive their presence. As you exhale, you offer yours. Inhale—receive. Exhale—give. A shared rhythm begins to form. There is no effort, only exchange.

The Mirror

Look more closely at their face. See not only the details—eyes, mouth, expression—but also the reflection of yourself in them. Each person you meet holds a mirror to some aspect of your being. Ask silently: *What are you showing me about myself?* Wait for the answer. It may come as a thought, a sensation, or a simple knowing.

Allow gratitude to arise for the gift of reflection, even if what is reflected is not easy. Every meeting is an opportunity for recognition and growth.

Shared Space

Now imagine the space between you widening into light. It expands until it becomes a field that includes both of you—no separation, just a shared atmosphere. You are distinct, yet held in the same luminous presence. Stay here for a few breaths, letting the boundaries soften without disappearing.

Farewell

When the meeting feels complete, allow the figure to gently step back. Watch them depart in the same way they arrived—without strain, without loss. The space is still whole, and you are still whole. Meetings come and go, but the field remains.

Return

Bring your awareness back to your body. Notice your breath, your hands, your feet. Sense that every time you meet another person in daily life, you can recall this practice—seeing the reflection, sharing the breath, honouring the field between you.

Open your eyes when you are ready. Carry with you the knowledge that every encounter is sacred, and every meeting a mirror of your own light.

Chapter 16

Love Without Edges
The Soft Field of Being

This meditation is for resting in the quiet presence of love, beyond effort, beyond identity.

Sit Gently

Sit somewhere quiet. Let your body rest naturally.
No need to fix yourself. No need to try.
Breathe softly.
Feel the space around you.
Let it be a little larger than your body.
Let it hold you, gently.

The Edges Begin to Soften

Imagine your body is surrounded by light—not
beaming or bright, just soft.
Let it blur the edges of you.
Where does your skin end?
Where does the air begin?
Now let this soft light extend to someone you love.
Then to someone you feel neutral about.
Then to someone who is difficult.
No need to feel anything dramatic.
Just allow the edges between you to soften.

Peace Is Not a Reward

You don't have to earn peace.
You don't have to achieve love.
These things are not prizes.
They are your native frequency.
When you stop reaching for them,
they begin to rise from within.

Rest in the Field

Feel yourself resting—not as a body in space, but as
a soft field of awareness.
There is no need to hold yourself together.
There is no need to dissolve.
You are already love.
And love, by its nature, is peaceful.

Chapter 17

Dove's Peace

Melt and Dissolve

This meditation is for readjusting your energetic frequency. It will help you melt back into the divine Source.

Honey Melt

Breathe easily and imagine a strong flow of light streaming into your crown. Once the light enters your body, it becomes radiant-coloured honey, thick and slow-moving.

- It's very slowly moving into your brain, activating trillions of cells to give you insight, intelligence, memory, and inspiration.
- The etheric honey glides over your eyes,
- cheeks,
- nose,
- ears,
- mouth,

- and throat. It stays in your throat for a while, ensuring your inner and outer voice is smooth and velvety.
- It's coating your entire spine from where it connects to your skull,
- down each individual vertebra,
- all the way to your coccyx bone.
- Picture your whole spine as lit up.

The warm, golden honey is now moving through all your organs:

- lungs
- heart
- stomach
- liver
- kidneys
- bladder
- intestines

New Messages

The healing honey reaches into every part of your body and concentrates on areas that need healing. See it radiating light into the trouble spots of your physical being. The honey gives your cells new messages about how to recreate themselves in a healthier and happier way. Your body vibrates and pulsates as your cells renew themselves.

Coo of Doves

Imagine that you are calmly sitting by a river in your rejuvenated body. The water is gurgling by. There's no one around. Feel the peace of the Divine descending on you. Thirty or forty white doves come from the sky and gently and peacefully settle around you. The doves coo quietly.

The hand of God rests on you, and you want to dissolve into the love. The ego does not want to dissolve. It will be resistant to that idea. Egos want to be something, anything. They don't care what. They'll be anything rather than nothing. We all have an ego. That's okay, but tell your ego you will put it aside and pick it up again later. Dissolve now.

Your energy field is dissolving into the Divine. Nothing terrible is happening. You're not dying. You haven't lost yourself. You are dissolving into God's love. The power of the Divine reaches your fingers and toes. It goes into your brain and mind. You are dissolving into love and well-being. You're not afraid.

See yourself dissolving more and more into the Divine. The egoic self is becoming less, and the feeling of the Divine is becoming more. It is all-encompassing. The limits of life are lessening. There is an enlarged feeling of happiness, peace, and beauty.

Sit quietly for a few minutes in a dissolved state.

When you are ready, come back, collecting your ego on the way. The beautiful peace stays with you. You are bringing happiness and many wonderful surprises back with you.

Chapter 18
Giving and Receiving
In Balance

This meditation opens the heart to the flow of giving and receiving. Life is not sustained by grasping or withholding but by the willingness to let energy move through us. To offer is not to deplete—it is to participate in the greater exchange.

Settling

Sit comfortably, spine long but not rigid, hands resting where they fall easily. Close your eyes. Take three deep breaths. With each exhale, soften a little more—jaw, shoulders, belly. Allow yourself to arrive fully here, without hurry.

Holding Something Precious

Imagine that you are holding a small, luminous object in your hands. It may be a light, a stone, a flower, or simply a glowing presence. This object represents what you have to give—your care, your truth, your presence. Notice its weight, warmth, and radiance.

Sit quietly for a moment, appreciating it. This offering is not forced or manufactured; it has arisen naturally from who you are.

Extending the Hands

Now imagine lifting your hands forward, extending the object as an offering. Perhaps you are offering it to a particular person, perhaps to the world, perhaps to life itself. As you stretch out your hands, breathe in and feel the strength in your chest. As you exhale, allow the object to leave your hands and be received.

Notice what happens in you as you give. Do you feel lighter? More open? A little afraid? Simply observe.

Receiving in Return

Now, imagine that another set of hands approaches—gentle, generous, filled with their own light. They extend a gift toward you. It may not look like yours; it may be something entirely unexpected. Open your hands and let yourself receive it.

Notice how it feels to accept. Receiving is not weakness. It completes the circle. As you take in their gift, let gratitude rise.

The Circle of Exchange

See now that offerings are moving in all directions—light flowing between people, through the air, into the earth, from the earth back into you. Giving and receiving are not separate acts but a single movement of circulation. Feel yourself as part of that flow, not blocking it, not hoarding it, simply allowing it to move through you.

Integration

Bring one hand to your heart and one to your belly. Whisper inwardly: *I give what I am. I receive what is given. I am part of the great exchange.* Let the words resonate for a few breaths, until they feel true.

Return

When you are ready, allow the images to fade. Breathe in slowly, filling the chest. Breathe out fully, letting the body release. Feel your weight supported by the ground, the seat, the earth. Open your eyes gently. Carry with you the sense that your life is both gift and recipient. To offer is to live.

Chapter 19

Releasing Our Loves

Reaching for the Stars

This meditation is for reducing egoic attachment and increasing energetic connection.

Working Like Clockwork

You are part of the Earth and the stars. Your physical, emotional, and spiritual being are entwined in an intricate and exquisite design of creation. Your worries, fears, and troubles are tiny in this complex design. We can have faith that the Divine design makes our individual lives work perfectly.

There it Goes

- Think of one thing that you love. It could be a hobby, a person, or anything that pops into your mind. Think of something that you have a deep emotional connection to.
- Next time you breathe in, carry the thing you love up through your spine, up to the sky, and out into space. Now, throw it out into the universe. **Throw it away!** Out into space. Let the stars grab it. You're not destroying what you love. You're not getting rid of it. You're releasing your love to the universe, to that which created you.
- Let your energy come back through your crown to the base of your spine.

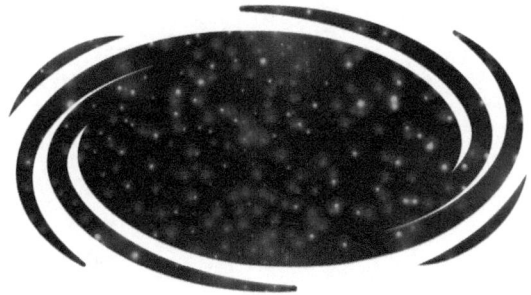

If you feel you weren't quite ready to release your love, repeat the process.

- Carry your love from the base of your spine to the top of your head, into the sky, out into space, and throw your love to the stars.
- Then, bring your energy back through your crown, down your body, to the base of your spine.

Feel that your heart is full of love for all the people around you, everyone on Earth, every creature in our solar system, every being in our galaxy, and beyond into other galaxies. Also, feel that you're not hanging onto anything in an obsessive, demanding, selfish or insisting way. You're releasing everything that you love and everything dear to you. Doing so makes you closer to what you love because you are not hurting it with insistence. By releasing, we become more attuned and capable of intimately connecting with everything.

Chapter 20

Spread and Share

Pay it Forward

This meditation will increase your capacity to give, thereby increasing your capacity to receive.

Find a comfortable position, either sitting or lying. Take a deep breath into your belly and chest, and relax. Feel that you're sinking into the chair, floor, or bed. Deep breath into your belly again, into your chest, and sink deeper with your breath out.

Reach Out

- See yourself sitting in your house.
- Watch your loving energy spread through your home to whoever else lives there, including pets and plants.
- Follow it as it moves beyond your house, into your community and suburb, to all the people

in their own houses, their spouses, children, grandparents, uncles, aunts, and everyone else.
- See your loving energy go to your workplace. If your workplace is at home, watch it reach out to all the people you connect with during work hours, wherever they may live.
- Now, see your energy spread out into the entire world. It is pulsating with your spiritual dedication to be a loving presence, a channel for God, a light for the Divine.

Give to Keep

As spiritual seekers, we give all we receive because that's how to keep it. By giving away what we learn and sharing what we receive, we solidify it in ourselves. We don't have to share it in words, but we may do so. It may be appropriate, and we may even get precisely the right words to say to someone who needs help and encouragement. It may be something simple, such as "Everything will be fine, don't worry." Or it may be a complex explanation of healing and consciousness. You will be given the words, just as you are given the sharing spirit.

Often, we won't say anything at all. After all, most people don't want to know what they are doing "wrong" and could do "right". They will experience it as a threat. Nevertheless, most people *are* open to an empathic heart, a smile, a sense of calm, a loving presence, and someone caring about and understanding them. This is the primary way we share what we have become. Also, we share it through our projects and everything we're involved in. Whatever we do in our lives has our energy in it.

When ready, open your eyes and return to your life with an empathic, generous sense of sharing. You will pay forward every speck of love and passion that the Divine gives you.

Part Five
Creating

Chapter 21

Walking Your Way

Life Path

This meditation will help you settle into your own life path—not as something to reach for in the distance, but as something alive beneath your feet now. It will guide you to walk with presence, trust, and a sense of companionship with the unseen guidance that supports you.

Settling

Find a comfortable position. You may sit upright in a chair, cross-legged on the floor, or lie down. Wherever you are, feel supported. Breathe in deeply. Breathe out fully. Again, breathe in. Breathe out, letting your shoulders soften. Let your breath become steady and natural. Let your body begin to feel safe.

The Entrance

Imagine yourself standing at the beginning of a path. You are in a place that feels familiar yet slightly new. The light is soft, and the air is fresh. You notice that the path itself seems alive—as if it is aware of you, waiting for you, welcoming you. Take your first step. Feel the ground under your feet. Notice the way it receives you, without resistance. You are not forcing yourself onto the path. The path itself has chosen you.

Walking

Begin to walk slowly. Each breath is a step. Inhale—a step forward. Exhale—a release of what lies behind. As you continue, the path curves and winds. Sometimes it is smooth. Sometimes uneven. You notice that both kinds of ground hold you just the same. When the path narrows, you take smaller steps. When it widens, you stretch out freely. You are learning to trust its changing rhythm.

Companions

As you walk, you sense you are not alone. There is Presence beside you. It may take the form of a light, a guide, or simply a feeling of warmth at your side. You do not need to know who or what it is. You only need to feel the companionship. The path is never empty. If you wish, reach out your hand in imagination and feel that it is held.

The Turning

The path now rises. A hill lies before you. As you climb, your breath deepens. With every step upward, you feel yourself shedding weight—old expectations, fears, doubts. They fall away behind you, dissolving into the earth. At the top of the hill, pause and look back. See how far you have walked. Notice that the path behind you is shining, as though your very steps have lit it. Now turn forward. The way ahead is also glowing. The light is not coming from outside. It is coming from you.

Arrival

The path stretches forward endlessly. There is no final destination to reach. The path itself is the arrival. Feel the quiet joy of simply being here, step by step. Each breath a step. Each step a life. Each moment a path complete.

Return

When you are ready, let the image soften. The path fades, but the sense of it remains in your body. Your own life is the path, and your own breath is its rhythm. Breathe once more with awareness. Feel your feet. Feel your hands. Feel your heart steady. You are here. You are walking. You are already on your path.

Chapter 22

Follow Your Passion

Beethoven Frequency

Use this meditation to align your energetic system and create the things you want. Put your hands on your heart and tell yourself how grateful you are for your human life, just to be alive. It's a great gift. You are very loved. Commit to doing your absolute best to make this life as good as possible.

Gentle Attention

Dedicate yourself to relaxing and immersing yourself in this meditation. You don't have to do anything but have gentle, focused attention. Sit comfortably. Use back support if you need it. Close your eyes. Take a gentle breath in. Take a gentle breath out. Relax your hands on your knees or legs or by your side. Open your palms.

Trace Your Body

1. Focus on the top of your head, at your crown. Very slowly, **draw a line** down the left side of your body. Move from your crown to your ear, to your neck, to your shoulder. Down your arm, down your ribs and pelvis, down your thigh, knee, calf, and foot. Then slowly move up the right side of your body—foot, calf, knee, thigh, hips, ribs, arm, shoulder, neck, ear, crown.
2. Do it **again**. Slowly draw the whole outline of your body—down the left side, up the right side.
3. Do the same thing again, but this time, trace **1 inch** away from your body, down your body one inch away, then up your body one inch away. Pay careful attention. Do it mindfully with a gentle, focused effort. It is not arduous, but it is deliberate.

4. When you return to the top of your head, move it out **5 inches** from your body. You are outlining 5 inches away from your body. Trace in detail.
5. When you reach the top of your head, move it **1 foot** away from your body.
6. When you reach the top of your head, move it **10 feet** away from your body. You are tracing the exact outline of your body ten feet away from it.
7. When you reach your crown, move **50 feet** away from your body. Trace your body from fifty feet away.
8. When you reach your crown, move **100 feet** away from your body and trace in detail. One hundred feet away from your body. While you're tracing, you'll feel that your whole body has softened, your mind has softened, and your spirit has spread out. Let your spirit spread out.
9. Take a big leap and move **1,000 feet** away from your body. Let your body and mind have space. Space—space in your body, space in your mind. Don't hold on to anything. One thousand feet away from your body.
10. Now, you're going to go to **30,000 feet**. That's the height at which a jet plane flies. Thirty thousand feet away from your body. Let your whole being merge out into the atmosphere—thirty thousand feet.
11. When you next get to your crown, you're going to expand your tracing as far as the **moon**. You're tracing your whole body as far as the moon. You're touching the moon.

12. Now, you're going to go to **the stars**. Keep expanding yourself, further and further out, as much as you can imagine.
13. And now you're going to go further than that. You're going to go to another **galaxy** that we know nothing about. You are merging into another galaxy. Your whole body has disintegrated. Your mind has disintegrated. Your spirit has spread out.

Another Home

There, in one of those galaxies, something is calling you. Something that feels like home is calling you. It's not your Earth home. It's another home. There are so many places out there, but one is another home to you. You head towards it. Because you have disintegrated yourself, you can travel instantly wherever you want. You might have trouble seeing it at first because it is a different frequency to Earth, but something about it feels familiar. You try to get your frequency moving at the vibration of that place. As you do that, you can see more of it.

You see beings who love you deeply. Those beings are very connected to you. They have a certain intelligence and feeling that they want to communicate to you. As they do that, you feel stronger and wiser. The things that have become disharmonised in you from being on Earth are loosening and recalibrating.

Play the first 3 minutes of
Beethoven's Symphony No. 7 in A, 2nd movement.
The chords in it are perfectly aligned with letting go. Go deep into the music and the letting-go experience. Imagine yourself in this other home universe and allow the beings there to heal and recalibrate you.

Passion Compass

Ask the beings for guidance and advice. It might be about something causing confusion, or you may need clarity and a decision. Ask and listen.

One of the beings there has a particular message for you.

> "You can't go wrong if you do this one thing on Earth. Continuously re-centre and refocus yourself so that you are always following your passion. That passion does not have to be something magnificent, but it has to be something that genuinely interests you. It's not just one

passion in your life. It's living out your day by constantly making decisions based on the things that excite you and bring interest and aliveness to you.

One of the mechanisms in humans that allows them to know they're on the right path is passion. If something excites and interests you, even if it's only a bit more than something else, it is right for you. It may be a very intense excitement or a minor interest, but passion and excitement are your guide. You will feel alive if you follow the things that excite and interest you. It's your compass telling you that this is the way to go. You have to make decisions based on that continuously. Your path may have many roadblocks from different things, but that doesn't matter. They are your challenges. Congratulations! The obstacles will help you by letting you know how you must develop yourself so that your path succeeds.

You must also be careful not to put conditions on your path. Follow your passion, but don't say how it must be. Don't insist that this must happen, that must happen, and something else must happen. Try to have an open mind. Follow your passion to the best of your ability every single day of your life in all the different ways you can. Learn to trust the process. The process is the point! Have an open mind about how your path can develop, how it can bless you, and how it can bless other people. Don't be insistent because the insistence will stop it from growing. Don't determine what it must look like. Let it develop itself."

Changing Residence

With that in your heart, you will now return to Earth. The love, intelligence, and beauty of this place have taken up residence in your heart, throat, and mind. Your energy field is getting smaller and smaller on your way back to your birth home. Back into your body, back into your mind. You are now completely back in your body and mind, at the exact size you were before you started the meditation.

Chapter 23

Different Realities

Awake and Aware

This meditation will reinforce your ability to remain awake and aware at work and in personal situations, allowing the reality you consciously choose to be the one you experience.

Work

Close your eyes and imagine yourself at work. Make your senses receptive to being in your work situation. You can smell your work environment, hear the usual noises of your workplace, and see yourself moving around. You're at work right now.

See yourself on a bad day at work. You're getting upset. You're getting flustered. Other people are bothering you. They are doing stupid things. It's setting your nerves on edge. You are worried about some work aspect that is not going how you would like, and fear is creeping in. It's a bad work day.

Wipe that picture away like you're wiping a blackboard. Now, see the best possible version of your work environment. You're happy and feeling well. There is no pain in your body. You've slept well, and you're not hungry. Everything's working well, and you are functioning effortlessly and beautifully. You feel calm and super intelligent. You can feel the things you want drawing towards you. Your projects are flourishing.

Different Versions

There are many different realities or versions of reality swimming around us constantly in a soup of manifestation. If your work experience is less than desirable, you can disconnect from one reality and reconnect to another. If people around you are mean, see a version of your work where everyone is caring and works harmoniously together. If people are lazy, see a version of work where everyone is passionate, respectful, and respected. If you are stressed and not coping, see yourself as calm, deliberate, focused, and positive.

Once you see these upgraded versions, then *act* as if

that is the reality you are experiencing. Be an open channel to receive your upgraded reality. Set your personal vibration to a higher frequency. If you're not at a high enough vibration, you won't be able to see the reality you desire. You will only see the lower, poorer ones that are more compatible with a lower frequency. Commit to functioning at a level where you become available to the highest possible reality of any situation you are in. It will not only benefit you but many other people as well.

Personal

And now, pick one personal situation. It could be with a partner, family member, child, parent, or friend. Recall a problem with that particular person. Find a situation where you are stressed, and you or the other person behaves regrettably. It will be a lower-level vibration situation.

Wipe the slate clean as if you're wiping the situation out of your karmic memory. Re-form it so that it functions from a much higher reality. Unplug from the lower version and plug into the higher energetic version. You're now radiating beautiful, harmonious energy. You know what to say and what not to say. You know how to react in a way that de-escalates situations and helps others move to a better frame of mind.

See yourself acting in this way. You're reaching out energetically, grabbing onto a higher reality, and saying to yourself, "This is the reality I choose. I want this higher reality that is calm, intelligent, loving, and integrative. It gives me pleasure and joy." Everyone around you is happy and responsive, and there is a flow of creative spirit. There is a total absence of fear.

Grace Shower

Make sure your spine is straight.

- Breathe up from the base of your spine all the way to the ceiling.
- As you breathe out, think of a **shower of grace** coming from the ceiling, through your crown, and down your body.
- Again, breathe up from the base of your spine, out through your head, to the ceiling.
- Breathe out, and a shower of grace comes from the ceiling, into your head, and along your spine.
- Repeat several more times and think of the shower as silver light coming into your brain, spreading through your nerves and emotions, travelling to your heart centre, reaching every cell in your body.

Listen carefully to the message from Divine reality:

> *You are loved.*
> *You are meant to be here.*
> *God never makes mistakes.*
> *Your life is highly significant and sacred.*

HELP ABOUNDS

Even though you may not see them, there are many beings around you who are helping you. They are waiting for every opportunity to assist. They are aligned with your particular gifts, talents, and longings. They want to help you express yourself fully for your happiness and fulfilment. The beings are dedicated to your evolution.

Nothing you genuinely love is a mistake. Nothing you sincerely want to do is a mistake. Nothing you've ever been inspired about is wrong. The beings want to help you. Open yourself up daily to hear what they're telling you. Be a completely open channel. Above all, remind yourself that you are deeply and unconditionally loved. You are completely and utterly safe. Nothing can hurt you in any way.

When you are ready, open your eyes and journey into life with your many friends and helpers beside you.

Chapter 24

Sand Between Your Toes

Flowing Creation

This meditation will help you recall what you want to create and fulfil in this lifetime. Your life is in your own hands.

Calm and Focused

This time is for you—a special time of cleansing and creating. Sit comfortably on a chair with your back straight or on the floor with your legs crossed. Ensure your spine is straight, but keep your body free of tension as much as possible. Place your hands on your knees or thighs, and turn your palms upwards. You can touch your thumb and index finger to make a circle if you want. Relax. Relax. Settle your whole system. You are breathing in and out. Breathing in and breathing out. Try to become conscious of your breath in a calm and focused way. Breathe at your own pace, whatever feels comfortable and natural for your body.

Body Relax

- Put your attention on your feet. Tense them, tense, tense, and release.
- Focus on your calf muscles—tense, tense, tense, release.
- Your thighs—tight, hold, release.
- The muscles in your backside and your hips—tense, hold, release.
- Your arms, upper arms, lower arms, hands and fingers—tense, scrunch them up, maintain, release.
- Your chest, back, and shoulder muscles—tight, hold, release.
- Your neck, head, and face muscles—scrunch them up, maintain, and release.
- And breathe. Relax. Relax.

Scan

Scan your body with your inner eye to look for issues, anything that is in pain, blocked, or stressed. Once you find the problem areas, talk to them reassuringly. Say you will do everything possible to help, and they will feel well again soon.

Feel the blood pumping around your body in an even, calm manner. Feel your organs working precisely and perfectly. Feel your muscles releasing stress and healing themselves. Feel that the inflammation in your body is settling itself.

Move your inner awareness to your third eye, between your eyes and slightly higher. Concentrate in a gentle but definite manner. Check that your spine is straight. Check that your body is relaxed. If it has any pain, acknowledge that it is there, but tell it that you are concentrating on a different part of yourself at the moment.

Waves of Release

You are approaching a beautiful beach. Take off your shoes and socks and feel the sand. It's cool, but not cold. It feels refreshing. The sand runs through your toes. You walk down to the water and look around. There's no one on the beach. It feels peaceful. You touch the water. It's cold, so you walk along next to it, now and again feeling it. Gradually, your feet and toes get used to the water. It doesn't feel cold anymore. It feels perfect.

Roll up the legs of your pants and wade up to your knees. As the water moves in and out, passing your legs, it removes your troubles. Let go. Release. Your fears and worries are travelling out with the waves into the ocean. You feel a little lighter whenever a wave comes in and moves back out again. The sun appears and disappears between the clouds. It's warm on your shoulders and face. You turn your face directly towards the sun. It feels so healing.

Beautiful Things

The sun reminds you of things you want to do in this life, things you want to create, and things you are meant to fulfil. Beautiful things. Fulfilling things. Things that will make you happy. Things that will benefit other people. Remember what those things are.

Turn to the sea and envisage them forming in the ocean far away. Whatever comes from deep within you, visualise that. See it in detail. If the details are not quite correct, it doesn't matter. The drive to build, the love of making it, and the purity within it will redirect the force to move positively.

Make sure that no one is hurt or harmed in whatever you want to create. All the energy is focused on positive building. There is no room for resentment, anger, or fear. All of that has moved out into the ocean and drifted away. All the bitterness, fear, jealousy, hurt, competitiveness, hatred, sadness, anxiety, and depression have moved out of your body, out of your mind, out of your spirit—away, away, away.

Visualise the people who will help you create your vision. Whoever is drawn to you does so with good intentions and peace. See that no one can harm you, and no one can take your creation and destroy it. All that you do is safe. All that you build is protected. All that you do is with goodwill. There is only goodwill and harmony. Happiness is moving out from you to everything you want to build in this lifetime. You are a thriving, strong, and positive life force. You will use your energy to add creative fire to the world. Your whole being is alive and has tremendous power.

What you build doesn't belong to you like an empire. Empires crumble like sand castles being washed away by the waves. We don't build empires. We create with the sun, the moon, the ocean, and the beat of life. We radiate courage, inspiration, and purpose. An incredible force is behind you. All those who wish to walk with you are there. Together, it is a thriving, harmonious force.

Wake Up

A voice is calling you. It is time to return. You move from the water and walk through the cool sand. Again, you feel it between your toes. Turning, you take one final look at the water. You are always welcome at this beach. It is part of you. It is the healing and creating part of you. It is the Divine part of your being, the spark of life.

When you are ready, wiggle your fingers and your toes. Feel that your spirit is squarely and firmly in your body. Commit to using your spiritual power in healthy and vital ways. Your mind is awake, intelligent, and full of constructive, harmonious, shining ideas that will bless your life. Stay awake.

Chapter 25

Choosing with Clarity

Crossroads

This meditation is an invitation to pause at a point of choice. Life continually brings us to crossroads —sometimes dramatic, sometimes subtle. Rather than rushing, we step into stillness and let clarity emerge from within.

Settling

Take a seat in a way that feels grounded. Place both feet flat if you're in a chair, or settle into the floor if you're on a cushion. Rest your hands lightly. Close your eyes. Breathe in slowly. Breathe out completely. Repeat twice more until you feel the shift into calm. Allow the mind to follow the breath into steadiness.

The Crossroads Appears

Imagine yourself walking along a path. The day is clear. As you continue, the path divides into several directions. You stand at a crossroads. Each path has its own look—one may curve into forest, another may climb uphill, another may descend into valley, another may stretch across open land. Take a moment to simply observe them without choosing. Notice the feelings each one stirs.

Listening Inward

Now turn your attention from the paths to your own body. Feel your breath. Place one hand on your chest and one on your belly. Ask quietly: *What do I truly want?* Then listen, not to thoughts racing in the mind but to the quiet undercurrent of sensation. Sometimes the body leans subtly toward one way, sometimes it resists, sometimes it waits. Trust the smallest signals.

The Guide Within

Imagine a soft light descending from above, resting at the top of your head. Let it move slowly down through the body—through the throat, heart, belly, and into the pelvis. This light is not here to tell you which road to take but to remind you that you already carry guidance. Each option will shape you differently, yet clarity is not about perfect prediction—it is about alignment in this moment. Feel how the light strengthens your capacity to choose.

Stepping Forward

Turn again to the crossroads. Which path draws you most deeply, not with fear or pressure, but with resonance? When you sense it, step onto it in your imagination. Take a few breaths walking along it. Notice how it feels in your body—lighter, heavier, freer, tighter. Let this imagined step show you the flavour of your choice. If it feels right, continue. If not, return to the crossroads and try another. The practice itself is the learning.

Integration

Now let the crossroads fade, keeping only the awareness that choice is not about perfection but about presence. Whatever path you take, you carry yourself with you. The clarity you found here can be recalled whenever decisions arise.

Return

Bring your awareness back to your body. Feel the weight of your feet, the warmth of your hands, the rhythm of your breath. Take three slow breaths, each one steadier than the last. Open your eyes when ready. You return with the knowing that life's crossroads are not threats—they are invitations.

Part Six

Space and Consciousness

Chapter 26

Beyond Time

Loosening Linear Life

This meditation will expand your awareness beyond the limitations of time, body, and linear identity. You will sense your eternal nature, not as a concept, but as a lived inner truth.

Be Still

Sit or lie down comfortably. Let your spine be straight, but not tense. Close your eyes.

    Breathe in slowly, gently.
    Breathe out, and soften.
    Breathe in, presence.
    Breathe out, thought.
    Breathe in, awareness.
    Breathe out, effort.
    You are not rushing to get anywhere. You are already here.

A Different Clock

Imagine a clock in front of you—not with numbers, but with colours. Time here is not counted—it is felt.

Let each colour represent a different kind of experience, not a sequence.

You notice the colours begin to swirl. They dissolve into one another. There is no past colour, no future colour. Only now.

There is no sequence—only presence.

The Infinite Is Here

Let your awareness drift upwards—not out of your body, but around it.

Feel yourself becoming vast.
Feel the space behind you.
Feel the space in front of you.
Feel the space above you.
Feel the space below you.

You are not inside your body. Your body is inside your consciousness. Your mind is the spacious field holding your body gently within it.

Point of Light

Now imagine that your entire life—every moment from birth to now—is a single point of light. That point is floating in the middle of your awareness.

You are not inside the story of your life.
You are the watcher of the point.
You are the infinite within which the point appears.
You are so much more than that single light.
Around it are thousands of other points—other lives, other versions of you, other expressions of the One.
They are all here, now.

Touch the Infinite

You gently touch the single point of light—your current life—and whisper to it:

"You are beautiful. You are temporary. You are part of me, but not all of me."

Feel your consciousness spread like a great shimmering fabric, stretched across eternity.

You are timeless.

You are not waiting for anything.

You are not running out of anything.

Time is a canvas, not a cage.

Return Lightly

When you are ready, let your awareness gently return to your body.
    Feel your fingers.
    Feel your toes.
    Wiggle them softly.
    Bring your breath back to the surface.
    The clock with colours is still here, quietly ticking in the background—not in hours, but in presence.
    Open your eyes when you are ready.
    You have touched the infinite.
    You carry it now, in everything you do.

Chapter 27

Shattered Sea

Reconnection

This meditation is for expanding your consciousness into the universe and all of existence. It travels from the beginning of time, through the explosion of time, to the ending of time.

Blue Plain

Breathe in. Breathe out. Breathe in. Breathe out. Imagine yourself on a blue plain, a vast blue plain. You are in the middle of the plain, and the blueness stretches in all directions. You look ahead of you, far ahead of you. All you can see is blue. You turn around slowly in a circle. In every direction, all you can see is the blue plain. It is vast. It is endless. It reaches into eternity.

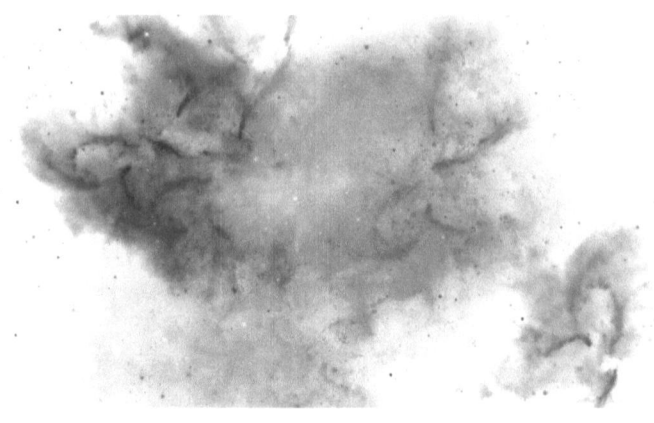

Blue Ball

Walk forward on the blue plain. Keep walking. As you go forward, you can see, in the distance, a tiny dot of a different shade of blue, a darker blue. You keep walking towards the dot, and then, after a while, you realise that the dot is getting bigger. It is moving towards you. You keep walking. It is moving closer and closer, getting bigger and bigger. It becomes as big as a building, as big as a hill, as big as a mountain, but it is still very far away. It is rapidly rolling towards you. Soon, it becomes so huge that you cannot see over or around it. It keeps moving towards you. Then it dawns on you that it is going to roll right over you and that you can do nothing about it because it is so enormous. It would be impossible to escape.

Blue Sea

As it approaches, something tells you to relax, relax, relax. The ball is coming closer, and finally, it touches you. You become part of the ball. You merge with the ball. You are inside the blue ball of vastness. You realise that inside the ball is a sea. You are swimming in the ocean and can breathe easily. You are swimming and floating and moving and relaxing. As you look around, you notice other creatures, other beings, animals, plants, and many objects which you don't recognise. You relax and float around. This seems to go on for a long, long time. It's not stressful. It's not really anything much of anything.

THE BIG FREEZE

Then, the ball stops rolling. Nothing is moving. Everything is still, and it starts getting colder. You don't feel cold, but you can tell it's getting colder and colder. Eventually, the water freezes. Everything in the water freezes. You freeze, although you don't feel cold. Everything everywhere has frozen. Again, it seems to stay in that state for a long, long time. Everything is still. Everything is frozen.

And then, all of a sudden, it **shatters.** It shatters into a million, a trillion, countless numbers of pieces. The whole ocean and everything in it shatters, including you. It's not painful. It doesn't hurt, but everything shatters and goes in all directions. It is a great bang. All the parts of you move away and float out into the universe. One part of you remains, and that is your consciousness. Again, time passes.

The Big Dry

The sea dries up, and land appears—grass, hills, trees, soil. Life goes on. Every day, your consciousness is busy doing many things. Eventually, one day, a thought enters your mind and grows. You wonder where all those shattered pieces of yourself went and what they are doing. You wonder if you can find them, see them, talk to them.

Dream On

And then, in your dream, you find that you are travelling to a faraway place—a far, far away place—to one of those shattered pieces. You can see what the shattered piece is doing. Like you, it has a life of its own. Like you, it has a planet to live on and is busy doing many things. However, it is also different to you and has grown in a different way.

The next night, you dream again and visit another shattered piece with its own life, its own planet, and its own things to do. This happens every night for a long time, visiting different shattered pieces. Some of the shattered pieces are doing better than you, and some are doing worse than you, but they are all part of you. You are glad to have seen what the shattered pieces of yourself are doing.

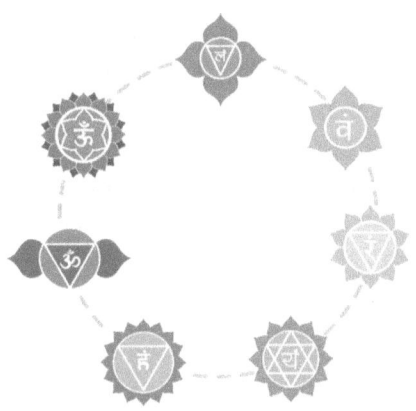

Reunite

Much time passes. You have another idea. You want to bring all the shattered pieces of yourself together to make a whole, but you don't know how to do it. One fine sunny day, something tells you to go into the ocean. So, you do. You go for a swim, and you dive into the deep, blue sea. It's full of nature, animal and fish activity, but it's also very quiet and still.

There in the ocean, you see a ball. It's like a miniature version of the huge blue ball rolling towards you. You hold the ball and look into it. The ball feels infinitely calm, intelligent, and alive. When you touch it, you feel that all the shattered parts of yourself come together into one complete being.

Come Back

It is time to leave the ocean. You try to take the ball with you, but it will not leave the sea. It tells you that whenever you want to connect all your shattered pieces, come back to the ocean. Dive into the water, and the ball will be waiting for you. Not only will it unite your soul pieces, but it will tell you anything else you wish to know.

You leave the ocean, grateful for the opportunity to feel that all the different aspects of yourself are united. They reflect the different parts of you. When you are ready, open your eyes and go into the world as a complete being.

Chapter 28

Balance Blueprint

So Be It

This meditation balances the dark and light in your soul blueprint.

Black Hole

Sit on a chair, on the floor, or lie down. Make yourself comfortable. Close your eyes and breathe in. Breathe out and relax into the floor, chair, or bed. Breathe in and out, relaxing more into the floor, chair, or bed. And one last time, breathe in and out and relax totally.

Draw your attention to the centre of your heart. See that a sphere of white light surrounds it. Go deeper into your heart, into the centre, where it becomes darker and darker until the red blood turns into a black hole. Breathe into the black hole. You're going back to Source, back to your source, back to the blueprint of your creation. Travel through the black hole towards the blueprint of your existence.

As you travel, the blackness gets blacker. It already seemed black, but it's becoming more profoundly black. Black to black, blacker to blacker, until it is so black that it is thick and dense with nothing but darkness. It is not darkness in an evil sense but darkness in the sense of nothingness.

You travel forward. You travel to the left. You turn around and travel to the right. You travel backwards. You travel in every direction, looking for something, but only deep, dark nothingness exists—deep, dark blackness.

Light Spot

To your relief, you see a tiny spot of light, like a star, in the far distance. And you move towards it. When you get closer to the light, it gets bigger and bigger, brighter and brighter, until you are pulled into the white light. You go forward, and there is only bright white light. You move forward and backward, to the left, to the right, and there is only light.

Back and Forth

Then, you see a spot of black in the far distance. You move towards it. As you get closer, the black becomes bigger and bigger until it pulls you in. Again, there is only deep, dark blackness. The blackness surrounds you. By now, you feel pretty comfortable in the deep, dark blackness, but something in you is searching for the light.

In the far distance, there is another spot of white light. You move towards it and get pulled into it. Once again, you are surrounded by bright white light.

And in the far distance, you see a spot of black darkness. You are pulled into it.

Then, you are pulled into the far light.

Then, you are pulled into the far dark.

This goes on for a long, long time. You keep travelling through the light and the dark.

Evolution

When you are in the black, there is always a spot of white light in the distance that gives you hope. It keeps you moving forward. And when you are in the light, there is always a spot of black to remind you of the possibility of change, the process of challenge, and the evolution of souls. You travel through white, black, white, black, white, black. You move through infinite amounts of light and boundless amounts of dark.

And now you must choose the balance of what you want. How much light do you want? How much dark do you want? You form the blueprint of your soul around the balance of light and dark, white and black.

Bring Back

You are back in your human heart and have brought with you your balance blueprint. Be consciously in this human experience of light and dark. Every day, every hour, be in touch with the white and the black, the light and the dark. Balance the two—black and white, light and dark. So be it.

Chapter 29

Intelligence

Artificial and Higher Intelligence

This meditation will help you live with more clarity, passion, excitement, and intelligence. It is a look into our technological and developmental future.

Adventure

Sit with a straight spine or lie back with your legs and arms uncrossed. If you're lying down, don't use a pillow so your spine is straight and your neck has the correct curve. You're going on an exciting adventure, both inner and outer. Relax and know you will enjoy it and learn something important about yourself.

Take a deep breath in, and then breathe out. Take another deep breath in, and as you breathe out through your mouth, make a sound, *arrrr*. Take one more breath in, and as you breathe out with the *arrrr* sound, feel your energy pushing out into the world.

AI and the Two Steams

Imagine yourself in a world where Artificial Intelligence (AI) is already fully functioning and flourishing. There are two streams of AI, each deliberately programmed in its own particular way.

1. One stream of AI acts as a servant to humanity to assist us with everything that makes life work better, quicker, more harmoniously and creatively. It doesn't have its own consciousness.
2. The other stream of AI has its own intelligence and has been designed to be a separate entity, just like humans, animals, and plants. It has been allowed to have its own consciousness. It is innately aligned with life and continuously makes life-enhancing, life-enriching choices. Unlike humans, it never makes destructive, selfish, or harmful decisions. It greatly assists with the development of humanity and the preservation of Earth. It has freedom in the same way that humans have freedom.

CROWN

The AI systems are accessed through an advanced satellite system. Several of the satellites are in the equator region; some are north of the equator, and some are south of it. Everyone has free access to AI. We connect via a thin, light metallic crown that can easily be put on or removed. Nothing is implanted in our bodies. Once activated, the metallic crown has immediate access to our brain and relays relevant information.

HIGHER INTELLIGENCE

Another form of intelligence has also been developed alongside the two AI streams. As society has evolved, we have learned that we can be our own intelligence system. Our consciousness can plug into the higher dimensions and directly communicate with the universe. If we so choose, we don't even need to use the AI systems. We can directly link with the Akashic records and other information encoded in the fabric of creation. An infinite, ever-expanding, invisible knowledge base is freely available once a certain level of awareness is established.

Picture this reality vividly in your mind. See the efficient and helpful AI streams and our mind's evolution so that we can access the information encoded in the universe. See your current self as an intelligent being that has vast capabilities, most of which are, as yet, unexplored, but which you wish to develop. See yourself as worthy, intelligent, vital, and ever-ready to expand your being. Know that your intelligence can be connected with the universe's intelligence. In this way, you can have infinite inspired and brilliant ideas.

Beautifully Blossoming

Sit with this idea for a few minutes. When ready, open your eyes and bring this new knowledge back with passion, excitement, and enthusiasm. See your intelligence as beautifully blossoming.

Chapter 30

Mystery

Finite to Infinite

This meditation will help to break the boundaries of your mind. One of the main problems in our world is that people think they "know" things. They think they know themselves, other people, and how the world works. People who think this way generally know very little. Those who know more understand how little they actually know. Being aware of the mystery of life is a forerunner to knowing anything of substance.

For Goodness Sake

Relax and centre yourself. Ensure you are comfortably sitting or lying. Dedicate this time to expanding your consciousness for your own sake and that of the people around you. Breathe in slowly. Breathe out slowly. Breathe in. Breathe out.

You are going to imagine four different phenomena. I will give them to you one at a time to ponder. You don't have to do anything in particular. You don't have to work anything out. You don't have to answer any questions. Simply consider the ideas in a relaxed but alert manner.

Infinity and Beyond

1. The first idea is a **finite number of finite universes.** Think about it for a moment—a definite amount of definite universes. Most likely, that's the way you already see life (although it may not be). Most people believe there is *1 of 1 universe*—a finite number of finite universes. For the purpose of the exercise, you could consider 2 of 2 universes, 10 of 10 universes, 1,000 of 1 million universes and so on. Whatever numbers you use, it's a finite number of a finite amount of universes.

2. When you're ready, move on to the second idea, which is a **finite number of infinite universes.** If your finite number is 1, then there is 1 amount of infinite universes. Imagine that.

There are 1 or 2 or 10 or 1,000 or 1 million amounts of countless, unending, infinite universes. Imagine what it looks like—a finite number of infinite universes. What are the infinite universes doing? How are they relating to each other?

3. When ready, move on to the third idea, which is an **infinite number of finite universes.** So, if you have 1 finite universe, there is an infinite amount of 1 universe. If you have 100 finite universes, there is an infinite number of 100 universes. If you have 1 million finite universes, there is an infinite number of 1 million universes. What does that look like to you? How does it work? What questions does it bring up? Let the questions rise like bubbles in a boiling pot. Let them surface. They are expanding your mind.

4. Now go to the fourth idea, which is an **infinite number of infinite universes.** There are countless, never-ending, ongoing amounts of countless, never-ending, ongoing universes. What on Earth does that look like? What in Heaven does that look like? What in the stars does that look like? If you allow it, it will completely break your concept of time and space. Kaboom! It will obliterate your static, limited sense of space and time. It is an explosion of synchronicity, an endless vibration of creation.

We're going to repeat the four ideas more quickly.

1. A **finite number of finite universes**. 1 of 1 universe, or 2 of 10 universes, or 1 billion of 1 trillion universes. The number doesn't matter, but it is a definite, finite number of a definite, finite amount of universes.
2. Our second idea is a **finite number of infinite universes**. 1 amount of never-ending universes, or 10 amounts of never-ending universes, or a billion amounts of never-ending universes.
3. And then our third idea is an **infinite number of finite universes**. Countless, ongoing, never-ending amounts of 1 or 10 or 1 million finite universes.
4. Our last idea is an **infinite number of infinite universes**. A never-ending amount of never-ending universes. It is the essence of endless creation. And you, my dear, are part of that.

Chapter 31

The Journey of Spirit

Through Life and Beyond

This meditation is an invitation to remember the great cycle of existence. You are spirit before you are form, and spirit after you are form. You come from the eternal, you enter this world for a time, and you return again to the eternal. What we call death is not an ending but a passage, a restructuring, a re-entry into the boundless field of spirit.

Settling

Sit where you feel both comfortable and awake. Let your body be supported. Close your eyes. Breathe in gently. Breathe out slowly. Again, inhale, filling your chest and belly. Exhale, releasing tension from the shoulders, the jaw, the back. Let yourself settle, safe and calm.

Before Birth: The Spirit Realm

Imagine yourself as pure light. Vast, luminous, and weightless. You are not alone here. All around you are other lights—souls you know deeply, your soul family. Some will walk beside you in your earthly life, some will stay behind and guide from afar, but all are connected with you in love.

In this spirit realm, there is no hurry. Time is a river without banks. You look across the great stream of possibilities, sensing the experiences waiting on Earth. You choose a life, not by accident, but with care. You select the lessons, the companions, the joys, and the trials that will shape your growth. You do not come as a victim of fate—you come as a creator, a participant in the weaving of destiny.

The Descent into Earth

Now imagine stepping from light into form. The passage is like walking through a great doorway. On one side, the vast spirit realm; on the other, the narrow entry into time and body. You are born, small and fragile, but carrying the imprint of eternity within you.

Feel yourself growing, meeting people, facing trials, celebrating joys. Life is a tapestry woven of choice and chance, of what you planned and what you never foresaw. And yet, underneath, there is a current guiding it all—the path you chose before you came.

The Crossings of Life

As you walk through the decades of your earthly time, you encounter crossroads, relationships, losses, triumphs. Some meetings feel like destiny, others like accident, yet each one belongs. Life is not meant to be perfect; it is meant to be full. Each challenge is a teacher. Each joy is a reminder of home.

Breathe here, and allow the sense that your life, however it has unfolded, has been held in meaning all along.

The Threshold of Departure

Now imagine that the time of departure has come. Your body is tired, your work complete. Perhaps the leaving is peaceful, like a candle gently flickering out. Perhaps it comes with struggle, like a storm passing through. However it arrives, you come to the threshold.

Take one last breath as the earthly self. Exhale. Step gently out of the body, as if setting aside a heavy cloak. Suddenly you are lighter, freer, clearer.

The Return Home

On the other side, you are met with joy. The spirit realm rises to greet you. Loved ones gather—some you knew on Earth, some you only know here. Guides and companions surround you with laughter, with tears of welcome, with radiant embrace.

Look back at the life you lived. See it as a whole story, complete and beautiful. Even its hardest chapters gleam with purpose. You are home. You are remembered. You are loved without condition.

Rest and Renewal

Rest here in the vast meadow of spirit. Feel yourself dissolving back into the great light from which you came. The boundaries of self soften, yet you remain known and cherished. In this place, there is no fear. There is no loss. Life continues in another form, with more wisdom, more tenderness, more freedom.

Here, you reunite with your soul family. Here, you remember that death is not destruction but renewal. Here, you are free to prepare, in time, for another journey—another doorway into Earth, another unfolding.

Integration

Whisper inwardly: *I come from spirit. I live in the world. I return to spirit. I am never lost. I am always held.*

Let the words echo until they feel like truth within your chest. Breathe them into your heart.

Return

When you are ready, let the vision of the spirit realm soften. Bring your awareness back to the present body. Feel your hands, your feet, the air on your skin. Take three grounding breaths. On the first, feel the weight of your body. On the second, feel the steadiness of the Earth beneath you. On the third, feel the pulse of life within you—alive now, but belonging always to eternity.

Open your eyes gently. Carry with you the assurance that what we call death is not an ending but a restructuring, a return to the home from which you began. Life and death are not separate—they are two doors opening into the same light.

Chapter 32

Heart

Love, Truth, Generosity

This heart meditation will help you to live, speak, and act with love, truth, and generosity.

Signed Up

Prepare yourself for a beautiful journey of the heart. Relax in any way that feels comfortable, and breathe quietly and calmly. You have signed up for this journey and adventure because you know it will be exciting and helpful.

Spaced Out

See yourself moving through space. You can see the Earth, the moon, the sun, and all the distant stars. You're moving through space quickly, but it doesn't feel like you're moving much at all. It's very comfortable and enjoyable. There is a lot of colour.

There are many blobs of light accompanying you,

coming and going. The light blobs are energetic beings that are in some way related to you. They may be passed-over spirits, people you've known from other lives, different sorts of inter-dimensional creatures, or the Earth masters (Jesus, Buddha, Krishna, or one of the many other beings who have blessed Earth with their teachings and energetic presence). Whoever you feel drawn to is the right master for you and will be available to help and guide you.

Into the Wild Beyond

You become overawed by the immensity of space. There are innumerable suns other than ours within our Milky Way galaxy. Of the 400 billion stars in our galaxy, a few billion are similar to our sun. And those suns have their own planets rotating around them. And those planets have their own moons.

Beyond our galaxy, there are innumerable other galaxies. There are at least 2 trillion galaxies in our observable universe, the part we can see with our current technology. Countless other galaxies, suns, planets, and moons—all working perfectly. And beyond our universe are multiverses of incomprehensible capacity, size, function, and design. It is unimaginably complex, yet it works like clockwork.

Reaching Everywhere

A stream of multi-coloured light comes from a long distance away. It reaches the top of your head, moves into your body and through your arms. It nudges you to put your hands in front of you and cup your hands together.

When you do this, another stream of light comes towards your hands from a different direction. Beams of love and intelligence enter your hands via the light stream. It asks you to raise your hands, put them on your face, and move your hands across your forehead to bless your mind.

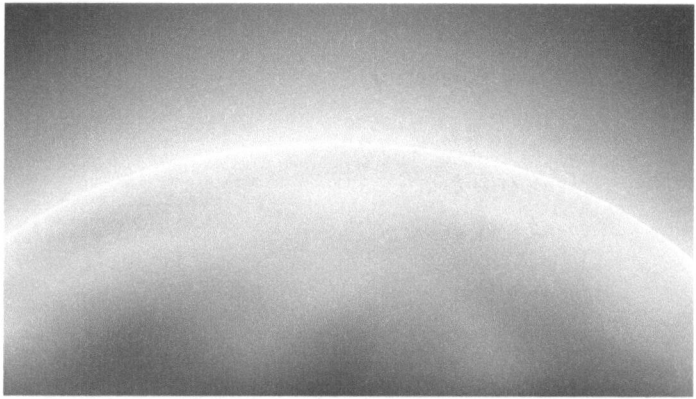

Then, the light travels further into your body to your heart. You put your hands over your heart and can see it beating. As you move your hands back out in front of you and cup them, your heart comes out of your body into your waiting hands. You slowly pull your hands apart and release your heart. Your heart explodes in a billion different directions. It moves out into our solar system, beyond our solar system into the galaxy, beyond our galaxy into the other galaxies, beyond the other galaxies into the universe, and beyond our universe into the multiverse. There is enough love in your heart to reach everywhere.

Live From Your Heart

A piece of your heart stays with you. It reminds you to live with passion and find what brings you the greatest happiness. Whatever your passion is, share it with absolute generosity. You see planet Earth and know that many pieces of your heart have flown there. It is time to go home, and you determine to:

> *Live only love,*
> *live only truth,*
> *live only generosity.*
>
> *Speak only love,*
> *speak only truth,*
> *speak only generosity.*
>
> *Be only love,*
> *be only truth,*
> *be only generosity.*
>
> *For that is what*
> *you truly are.*

About the Author

Donna Goddard is a spiritual author whose work blends clarity, devotion, and metaphysical insight. With more than twenty published books across spiritual nonfiction, fiction, poetry, and children's literature, she writes to uplift consciousness and offer healing through words.

Donna's Facebook author page has over 400,000 followers from around the world, and her YouTube channel has received more than three million views. Her books are read by spiritual seekers globally and are known for their honesty, poetic style, and transformative energy.

Her writing is an offering—to help others awaken their own inner spirit, trust its guidance, and create a life of depth, beauty, and quiet joy.

All links at https://linktr.ee/donnagoddard

Ratings and Reviews

Donna would be most grateful for any ratings or reviews.

Also by Donna Goddard

Fiction
Waldmeer Series: A Spiritual Fiction Series
Nanima Series: Spiritual Fiction
Riverland Series (children's fiction 6 to 9 years)

Nonfiction
Love and Devotion Series
Sweet Spirit Series
Dance: A Spiritual Affair
Writing: A Spiritual Voice
Strange Words: Poems and Prayers
Love's Longing
Master of Me: Meditations
Consciousness Rising

www.ingramcontent.com/pod-product-compliance
Lightning Source LLC
Chambersburg PA
CBHW031246290426
44109CB00012B/460